FIRE ON THE MESA

By
Tracey L. Chavis
and William R. Morris

ISBN 1-887805-18-4

Authors
Tracey L. Chavis
William R. Morris

Mesa Verde Centennial Series Editor
Andrew Gulliford

Content and Copy Editor
Elizabeth A. Green

Design and Layout
Lisa Snider Atchison

Mesa Verde Centennial Series Editorial Committee
Lisa Snider Atchison, Tracey L. Chavis,
Elizabeth A. Green, Andrew Gulliford, Tessy Shirakawa,
Duane A. Smith and Robert Whitson

Printed in Korea

To the memory of John Kenoyer,

a true friend

and fellow firefighter.

A message from the Superintendent
of Mesa Verde National Park

Our centennial celebrates an important moment in Mesa Verde National Park's history. It is an opportunity to share stories of what led to establishment of the park on June 29, 1906, and its designation as a World Heritage Cultural Site in 1978. This is a time to reflect upon its past and share hopes and visions for the next 100 years.

As Mesa Verde National Park nears its 100th birthday, it is important to remember that the archaeological sites it protects have been here far longer. Their survival is a credit to the skilled Ancestral Puebloan masons who created them 700 to 1600 years ago.

Following the Puebloan people's migration south to the Rio Grande area around 1300, the Utes continued to occupy the Mesa Verde area. They remain today and were responsible for the protection and preservation of Mesa Verde prior to its establishment as a national park. The park and the American public owe much to all these surviving indigenous people.

More than 100 years before its establishment as a national park, non-native people began exploring and documenting the archaeological sites at Mesa Verde, including Spanish explorers, geologists, ranchers, miners, photographers, naturalists, and archaeologists. They shared the story of fantastic stone cities in the cliffs, attracting more and more visitors to the area.

Prior to 1914, the 25-mile trek from Mancos Canyon to Spruce Tree House took an entire day, traveling the first 15 miles by wagon and the next 10 miles on foot or by horseback. This included a nearly vertical climb to the top of Chapin Mesa. Today more than one-half million people visit Mesa Verde National Park each year – a considerable increase over the 100 visitors documented in 1906.

"Leaving the past in place" is just one of the unique ideas pioneered at Mesa Verde. In 1908, when archaeology mainly consisted of collecting artifacts for distant museums, Jesse Walter Fewkes repaired, but did not rebuild, Spruce Tree House for visitation. He documented the excavation and created a small museum to house its artifacts. That tradition is continued today and Mesa Verde is recognized worldwide as a leader in non-invasive archaeology – studying and documenting sites without shovels to disturb the past. With the involvement of the 24 tribes affiliated with Mesa Verde and ongoing research, we continue to learn more about the stories that Mesa Verde National Park preserves.

Our centennial will celebrate 100 years of preservation and honor all who have gone before us. This centennial book series was created to tell some of their stories, of discovery, travel, transportation, archaeology, fire and tourism. These stories have contributed to our national heritage and reinforce why we must continue to preserve and protect this national treasure for future generations.

Enjoy the celebration. Enjoy the book series. Enjoy your national park.

– Larry T. Wiese

About the Mesa Verde Museum Association

Mesa Verde Museum Association (MVMA) is a nonprofit, 501 (c) 3 organization, authorized by Congress, established in 1930, and incorporated in 1960. MVMA was the second "cooperating association" formed in the United States after the Yosemite Association. Since its inception, the museum association has provided information that enables visitors to more fully appreciate the cultural and natural resources in Mesa Verde National Park and the southwestern United States. Working under a memorandum of agreement with the National Park Service, the association assists and supports various research activities, interpretive and education programs, and visitor services at Mesa Verde National Park.

A Board of Directors sets policy and provides guidance for the association. An Executive Director assures mission goals are met, strengthens partnerships, and manages publishing, education, and membership program development. A small year-round staff of five, along with more than 15 seasonal employees, operates four sales outlets in Mesa Verde National Park and a bookstore in Cortez, Colorado. The association carries nearly 600 items, the majority of which are produced by outside vendors. MVMA currently publishes approximately 40 books, videos, and theme-related items, and more than 15 trail guides.

Since 1996 MVMA has been a charter partner in the Plateau Journal, a semi-annual interpretive journal covering the people and places of the Colorado Plateau. In addition, the association has been a driving force in the Peaks, Plateaus & Canyons Association (PPCA), a region-wide conference of nonprofit interpretive associations. PPCA promotes understanding and protection of the Colorado Plateau through the publication of joint projects that are not feasible for smaller associations.

Mesa Verde Museum Association is also a longtime member of the Association of Partners for Public Lands (APPL). This national organization of nonprofit interpretive associations provides national representation with our land management partners and highly specialized training opportunities for board and staff.

Since 1930 the association has donated more than $3 million in cash contributions, interpretive services, and educational material to Mesa Verde National Park. MVMA's goal is to continue enhancing visitor experience through its products and services, supporting vital park programs in interpretation, research and education.

Visit the on-line bookstore at mesaverde.org and learn more about Mesa Verde National Park's centennial celebration at mesaverde2006.org. Contact MVMA offices for additional information at: telephone 970-529-4445; write P.O. Box 38, Mesa Verde National Park, CO 81330; or email info@mesaverde.org.

The Center of Southwest Studies

The Center of Southwest Studies on the campus of Fort Lewis College in Durango, Colorado, serves as a museum and a research facility, hosts public programs, and strengthens an interdisciplinary Southwest college curriculum. Fort Lewis College offers a four-year degree in Southwest Studies with minors in Native American Studies and Heritage Preservation. The Center includes a 4,400-square-foot gallery, the Robert Delaney Research Library, a 100-seat lyceum, and more than 10,000 square feet of collections storage. The new $8 million Center of Southwest Studies building is unique among four-year public colleges in the West, because the facility houses the departments of Southwest Studies and Anthropology, and the Office of Community Services, which helps Four Corners communities with historic preservation and cultural resource planning.

The Colorado Commission on Higher Education has recognized the Center of Southwest Studies as a "program of excellence" in state-funded higher education. Recent gifts to the Center include the $2.5 million Durango Collection ®, which features more than eight hundred years of Southwestern weavings from Pueblo, Navajo and Hispanic cultures.

The goal of the Center is to become the intellectual heart of Durango and the Southwest and to provide a variety of educational and research opportunities for students, residents, scholars and visitors. Strengths in the Center's collections of artifacts include Ancestral Puebloan ceramic vessels, more than 500 textiles and dozens of Southwestern baskets. The Center's holdings, which focus on the Four Corners region, include more than 8,000 artifacts, 20,000 volumes, numerous periodicals, and 500 special collections dating from prehistory to the present and with an emphasis on southwestern archaeology, maps, and original documents. These collections include nearly two linear miles of manuscripts, unbound printed materials, more than 7,000 rolls of microfilm (including about 3,000 rolls of historic Southwest region newspapers), 600 oral histories, and 200,000 photographs. Contact the Center at 970-247-7456 or visit the Center's website at swcenter.fortlewis.edu. The Center hosts tours, educational programs, a speakers' series, and changing exhibits throughout the year.

Center of Southwest Studies website: http://swcenter.fortlewis.edu

About the publisher

The publisher for the Mesa Verde Centennial Series is the Ballantine family of Durango and the Durango Herald Small Press. The Ballantine family moved to the Four Corners region in 1952 when they purchased the *Durango Herald* newspaper.

Durango has a magnificent setting, close to the Continental Divide, the 13,000-foot San Juan Mountains, and the 500,000-acre Weminuche Wilderness. The Four Corners region encompasses the juncture of Colorado, Utah, Arizona, and New Mexico, the only place in the nation where four state borders meet. Residents can choose to ski one day in the San Juans and hike the next day in the wilderness canyons of southeast Utah. This land of mountains and canyons, deserts and rivers is home to diverse Native American tribes including the Southern Utes, Ute Mountain Utes, Jicarilla Apache, Hopi, Zuni, and the Navajo, whose 17-million-acre nation sprawls across all four states. The Four Corners is situated on the edge of the Colorado Plateau, which has more national forests, national parks, national monuments, and wilderness areas than anywhere else on earth.

Writing and editing the newspaper launched countless family expeditions to Ancestral Puebloan sites in the area, including spectacular Mesa Verde National Park, the world's first park set aside for the preservation of cultural resources in 1906 to honor America's indigenous peoples. The Ballantine family, through the *Durango Herald* and the *Cortez Journal,* have been strong supporters of Mesa Verde National Park and Fort Lewis College.

Arthur and Morley Ballantine started the planning for the Center of Southwest Studies at Fort Lewis College in 1964 with a $10,000 gift. In 1994 Morley began the Durango Herald Small Press, which publishes books of local and regional interest. The Press is proud to be a part of the 100th birthday celebration for Mesa Verde National Park.

Durango Herald Small Press website: www.durangoheraldsmallpress.com

TABLE OF CONTENTS

ACKNOWLEDGMENTS

The following people helped make this book possible
through their expert knowledge and advice, proof-reading, and support:
Scott McDermid, Ross Wilmore, Jim Kitchen, Julie Bell, Guy Keene, Larry
Nordby, Lynn Dyer, Jane Anderson, Gay Ives, Dave Stoeger, Charlie Peterson,
Alisa Gardiner, Allan Loy, Tim Oliverius, Mark Mullenix, James Chavis, Kathy
McKay, George San Miguel, and Shirley Jones

EDITORIAL ASSISTANCE

Sandra Scott, Patricia Flint Lacey, Jennifer Usher

PREFACE

As visitors drive into Mesa Verde National Park today it appears very different than it did just a few years ago.

Once past the campground they begin to see the charred skeletons of trees along both sides of the road. From the campground until Park Point, the scars are all from the Bircher Fire.

Approaching the Far View area, visitors can see that grasses and brush are growing back well amid blackened tree skeletons. Damage in this area is from the 1996 Chapin 5 Fire.

After passing the Visitor Center and heading down to Chapin Mesa visitors see the most dramatic effects of fire. For the first mile or so the trees are still dense, lending a sense of what the entire area used to be like when visitors couldn't see off the road very far at all. After that first mile, the burned trees from the Long Mesa '02 Fire come into view on both sides of the road.

This opening up of the forest poses another problem. Now that people can see through the forest, they want to explore there. However, the backcountry is closed at Mesa Verde because there simply aren't enough staff to protect all the archaeological sites, especially now that some are much more exposed than ever before.

Visitors to Wetherill Mesa see extensive damage to structures as well as the forest.

Fires have changed the landscape of Mesa Verde National Park for decades to come, perhaps longer.

I

The Summer
of 2000

**The Bircher Fire started by a lightning strike on private land,
and grew quickly.**

I t is said that lightning doesn't strike twice in the same place. However, two strikes within close proximity to Mesa Verde National Park were enough to make the summer of 2000 the worst fire season on record.

At 12:44 p.m. on Thursday, July 20, a trail crew working at the Mancos Valley overlook near the northeast boundary of the park reported a "smoke" to the chief ranger's office. The single-tree fire was actually outside the park on private land owned by John Bircher. Lightning had struck the tree earlier in the week; it smoldered silently until conditions were just right for a blowup. The tree exploded in flame, and within minutes the fire grew, gathered strength, and headed for Mesa Verde.

At 1:19 p.m., the Mancos Volunteer Fire Department asked for assistance. By 1:36 p.m., other local engines began arriving on the scene. The National Park Service responded quickly and decisively. Just before 2 p.m., Fire Management Officer Tim Oliverius recommended the park be evacuated and called for a regional fire management team.

The fire was burning just below the winding, 20-mile park entrance road – the only access into and out of Mesa Verde National Park. Flames might block the park's only escape route. Visitors had to be evacuated immediately. When park visitation is at its peak in late July and early August, the number of visitors and employees can easily exceed 6,000 on any given day. With people spread out all over the park, evacuation would be difficult at best. In a little more than two hours, law enforcement rangers and Mesa Verde employees managed to evacuate

Mesa Verde National Park/Laura Martin

Evacuation, 3 p.m. Evacuation of the park was completed in less than two hours, thanks in part to the highly visible, dramatically growing smoke column.

everyone – quite an accomplishment.

As the initial evacuation of visitors progressed, there was a steady line of traffic heading out of the park. It was hard for them to take their eyes off the growing column of smoke that drew ever closer, the nearer they got to the entrance. The collective sigh of relief was nearly audible as visitors realized they were past the fire and nothing blocked their exit onto the highway.

Local fire departments, the Mesa Verde National Park helicopter, and a hand crew of park employees trained in wildland firefighting initially attacked the blaze.

A plane drops retardant on the fire, attempting to stop its spread. Planes and helicopters were called for immediately, and arrived by early evening. In the year 2000, fire resources were spread thin throughout the West.

Their main role was to clear a line of all vegetation around the fire. With no fuel to burn, the fire might be contained. But by nightfall the Bircher Fire had grown to more than 500 acres. The 20-person crew struggled through the night against rugged terrain, drought-stricken vegetation, and an unpredictable fire in their initial attempts to contain the blaze.

Oliverius and other Mesa Verde officials were concerned about the potential for this fire to spread and they had every reason to worry. Prolonged drought had been causing extreme fire danger all summer. They knew this fire could quickly rage out of control. It would require resources and skills beyond those available locally.

Regional and national fire management teams, known as Incident Management Teams or IMTs, include highly qualified people in such areas as fire behavior, weather prediction, air and ground operations, planning, information management, financial record-keeping, supply and resource coordination, training, and medical operations. But mobilizing a team takes time. As the hand crew struggled through the night to contain the fire, the regional IMT was being assembled. It wouldn't reach the park until early the next morning.

Meanwhile, the park's senior management remained in charge. Oliverius, a tall, quiet man, had waged a long battle to increase tree thinning in housing areas as well as around archaeological sites. He worked for Chief Ranger Charlie Peterson, who in turn answered directly to Superintendent Larry Wiese. Wiese signed all the

BIRCHER EVACUATION

Michael Groomer, a former interpretive ranger at Mesa Verde National Park from 1995 to 2001, remembers well the evacuation of park residents during the Bircher Fire. Saturday night, July 22, Michael was busy watering down the roof of his park house when a couple of his neighbors – firefighters – came home and quickly loaded up their dog and a few personal items to take out of the park. There had been no call for evacuation of residents, but the firefighters were busy battling the blaze all day and didn't know when they might have the chance to get back into the park for belongings, and of course they needed to make arrangements for their pet. Michael took their actions as a sign that it was dangerous to stay in park housing and concluded it must be time for everyone to leave.

Michael Groomer

He called the chief ranger's office around 9 p.m. to tell them he was leaving. He was told they would prefer that he wait until morning but Michael insisted he was leaving, so the rangers asked him to wait for an escort. By the time law enforcement rangers arrived in the housing area, several other residents were packing and wanted to leave as well. The cars joined a caravan led by the rangers, stopping at the Far View housing area to pick up several ARAMARK employees. As they were about to resume their trip out of the park, the rangers were notified that the fire had breached the road, making it unsafe to attempt an evacuation at that time.

Residents made their way back to their homes, leaving their vehicles packed. If Michael was any indication of the general mood, no one slept that night. They were feeling trapped and scared. Michael credits law enforcement rangers with doing a good job to get everyone calmed down, but with the smell of smoke thick in the air there was no denying their situation and they weren't happy. Throughout the night Michael could look out his window and see the glow of the fire, highlighted occasionally by flames shooting into the sky. Not knowing how far away the fire was only intensified his worry. By the next morning ashes were falling in the housing area.

All day Sunday, firefighters fought the Bircher Fire as it jumped back and forth across the park road, holding the residents hostage for yet another sleepless night. Early Monday morning, about 5 a.m., Michael heard a knock at his door. One of his fellow rangers told him the evacuation was back on and they needed to get out of the park before fire activity would increase as the morning warmed up. Residents were told to drive on the center line, well away from either edge, and not to stop!

Michael compares the drive down the hill to driving through a horrible burning moonscape. The landscape was charred and smoking. The wooden posts on which the guardrails are usually mounted made portions of the roadway look as if it were lined with giant luminarias. The twisted metal guardrails themselves were lying in the road along with rocks of all sizes and other debris.

Following their evacuation, park residents stayed in local motels for about a week until park fire officials declared it was safe for them to return to their homes. When they were ordered to evacuate once again, less than two weeks after the first evacuation, residents were packed and ready to go. As Michael drove down the hill for the second time, he stopped at Park Point, the highest point in the park, and called his parents on his newly acquired cell phone. He described the scene before him, saying it was as if he were looking down on millions of little lights from a huge metropolis.

Michael returned to find his house undamaged after the twin evacuations in 2000, but he couldn't shake the feeling that his house was in danger. He stayed at Mesa Verde one more year, then left for a new position in Alaska. Ironically, the house Michael occupied while at Mesa Verde was one of the two residences lost to the Long Mesa '02 Fire the next summer.

Today, Michael professes a great love for Mesa Verde National Park and considers it the most special place he has ever lived. Still, the fires of 2000 robbed him of something – the feeling of security he always had when he lived in the park. Now he is very aware of his surroundings and particularly of escape routes. He doesn't put himself in situations with only one way in and out. Maybe more than anything else, Michael hates lightning storms and still doesn't sleep well after them.

Mesa Verde National Park

Groomer's house at Mesa Verde. It burned the year after he left during the Long Mesa Fire in 2002.

The Bircher Fire, July 20, 2000, from Mancos Overlook. This helicopter was sizing up the fire, which was already beyond its ability to stop it. The fire spread into the park, moving south and west. Residents watched the fire into the night from county roads in Mancos.

important documents relating to the fire and was the official representative of the park, but regularly consulted his 12-member senior management team. Since the Bircher Fire began on private land, Mancos Volunteer Fire Chief Lyle Cox also was brought into the process.

Transition from one command to the other is always the most dangerous time on a fire, briefly shifting some attention away from actual firefighting. The incident commander, Joe Hartman, would normally have observed the fire, waited for additional resources to arrive, put together a plan, and taken the fire over the next day. But the Bircher Fire was spreading rapidly, quickly outpacing local resources. Hartman's team took over immediately, signing delegations of authority with the park service, Bureau of Land Management and Montezuma County Sheriff that morning. That evening, a separate agreement was signed with Ute Mountain Ute officials.

The Bircher Fire's intensity and unpredictability in the early morning indicated it would not be a "routine" fire by any means. The newly arrived team hit the ground running. After a briefing by the commander, they established a command post, ordered additional resources, created an initial action plan, and got the firefighters back out on the line.

The first couple of days on a fire are often the most chaotic. The team is just arriving – they have to meet with local officials, scout the fire and size it up, help draft the transfer of authority and get it signed so it is their fire to run, determine how many additional crews, engines, helicopters, tankers, and other resources to order and get them on the way to the fire. They must coordinate with air attack,

One of the many helicopters working the Bircher Fire, drawing water from a local landowner's pond.

The Bircher Fire from Park Point on Friday, July 21, 2000.
The fire's plume reached 50,000 feet, and
ashes dropped in Pagosa Springs 70 miles away.

Mesa Verde National Park

Fire affected tourism directly but also had impacts on the entire valley.

Camp at the fairgrounds where the supervisors remained close to communications and other functions. The majority of the other firefighters' tents were outside.

find out what has been done so far, what resources are available and their capabilities. They have to establish a base camp and order everything to set that up – catering service, latrines, hand-washing stations, food and drinks, supply trucks, radios and so on. They must create their first incident action plan, the first communications plan, and the medical unit plan. Until most of the resources arrive, there is constant change: establishing the credentials of the new arrivals, adding them to the action plan, making sure they have the proper equipment and verifying they have followed work/rest guidelines.

Despite the appearance of chaos with so much happening, this initial staging is in reality a well-oiled machine. Team members have done this many times before. Everyone has a job, knows what it is and how it fits into the bigger picture, and gets it done.

The official report for Friday, July 21, 2000, described early priorities, particularly in the oak brush and pinyon pine that blankets Mesa Verde.

> Only after the team had determined we could maintain **L**ookouts, **C**ommunications, **E**scape routes, and **S**afety zones, were crews deployed onto the line. Crew deployment could not be done prior to establishment of **LCES**. This was due to continuous fuels, extremely steep slopes, and very hot and dry weather. Over the last 25 years, many firefighters have been killed in these fuel types under similar conditions.

The 1,000-plus people involved in fighting the Bircher Fire took up residence at the Montezuma County Fairgrounds, seven miles west of the park entrance on U.S. Highway 160. This was the only facility in the area large enough to establish a base of operations for an effort of this magnitude. As the Bircher Fire grew in scope and complexity, so did the firefighting effort. The temporary fire camp was

Engines from far and wide. These engines were pre-positioned at Far View to protect the lodge, visitor center and other buildings. These engines are not used in fighting wildland fire in rough, remote terrain. They stand by to protect buildings if fire threatens them.

in many ways like a small town. It had a sort of mini-zoning – there were designated areas for camping, dining, briefings, supply trucks, and the myriad of other functions needed to keep a small town operational. Morning briefings were held in the same place, at the same time, daily. The offices were set up to encourage efficient work flow. Overnight, scores of phones and phone lines were brought in to some of the most unlikely places, along with copiers and fax machines. By the first day there was even a small phone book containing all the new fire camp phone numbers and any others needed. Dozens of coolers throughout camp contained water, juice, and Gatorade. Desks, tables, chairs, easels, office supplies, tents, and sunshades were put up for outdoor work areas. There were supply trucks, huge catering trucks to prepare three meals a day for 1,000-plus people and a dining area with tables and chairs to accommodate them. Shower units were in big semitrailers, one side for men, the other for women. Hand-washing stations were set up at the start of the food line. And almost all of the camp was in place in less than 48 hours.

A huge fleet of vehicles was put into service – fire engines, chase trucks, crew busses, support vehicles, 4-wheel-drive vehicles for getting crews out to remote locations – and a ground support crew to keep track of them, check them out, and inspect for damage. Of course fuel trucks and mechanic trucks also were needed to keep them running.

When the crews came in off the line to eat dinner, they were filthy, their faces, hands, and clothes all the same color: black. Most were great about washing their faces and hands before dinner but it seemed to be a badge of honor to let their clothes get as dirty as possible during a fire. It shows the world just how hard they have been working.

It is difficult to calculate the physical and emotional toll a major fire takes on those fighting it, as well as on local residents. Many park employees had grown up

A dirty face at dinner.
Keeping the fighters well-nourished is a key to their success.

Firefighters working to contain this area, during a time of day when active flame should be less visible.

After a long hard day, active flame at night is very discouraging. This photo was taken after 11 p.m., during the first day of the fire.

Firefighters wait to receive instructions before going out on fire lines.

in the area and spent their entire careers at the park. People had met, fallen in love, gotten married, and raised their children at Mesa Verde. It wasn't just the place they worked, it was their home. It was overwhelming to them to stand by helplessly when it might go up in smoke.

Julie Bell is an archaeologist and a trained firefighter. She goes out with the crews as they cut fire lines, walking a little ahead of them as she looks for archaeological sites and flagging them. When possible, crews avoid the sites – mostly rubble mounds – and build the fire line around them. A 1996 fire had revealed hundreds of previously unrecorded archaeological sites, so speculation ran rampant about the possible number of additional sites the Bircher Fire might uncover. At a press conference, a journalist asked Bell if she was excited about that prospect. She was speechless. She broke down and cried, saying there was nothing exciting about this fire. Her home was in the park, she had had to evacuate her dog and her most prized possessions, she was operating on very little sleep, as was everyone, and she was afraid there would be nothing left of the park she loved.

Understandably, many park employees wanted to be involved in the suppression effort or overhead support. It felt better to do something – anything – to stay busy instead of driving themselves crazy with worry. However, the benefits of putting an Incident Management Team in charge were clear. They are well trained and highly qualified to deal with the fire and the myriad of additional issues. Fires like Bircher impact so many people in countless ways that they become highly charged, emotional events.

Everyone wanted the fire put out, but stopping it would not be easy. The longer it burned, the angrier some people became. Some even speculated that fire-

TRACKING THE FIRE

SATURDAY, JULY 22, 2000

...An early reconnaissance flight indicated the fire had been active all night and that a historic cabin had been burned. The fire had spread onto the Ute Mountain Ute's Reservation. At 0930 hours, the inversion began to lift. Active fire spread again to the south and west. Steep terrain with little or no access limited aggressive ground firefighting techniques...The fire was spreading to the east, west, and south throughout the day. Again, the small gains in the containment of the fire were found by utilization of the aircraft assigned to the fire...What aircraft were available were used to prevent spread across the Mancos River Canyon to the east...An additional 4,000 acres were burned.

SUNDAY, JULY 23, 2000

The inversion had already lifted by 0600 and the plan for the day was obsolete by 0700. A Type I Team (Lohrey), ten more crews, 15 Type VI engines, and three strike teams of structural engines were ordered. At 0730, the fire was making a significant run toward Morefield Village. At 1100 the fire was spotting across the park road and all personnel were ordered to retreat to Morefield Village. The fire was making a run to the west of Morefield Village on Prater Ridge. Morefield Village was successfully defended due to actions during the previous days including fuel reduction and the establishment of a sprinkler system...The Morefield Village area provided more than adequate safety zones. Once the fire front passed, quick follow-up with engines saved a comfort station that had ignited...As the day progressed, new

Mesa Verde National Park

Firefighters wrapped Park Point Fire Lookout with fire shelters to protect the wooden elements of the building. It worked! This CCC building is still used as the park's fire lookout.

heads developed and fire spread again to the west and south with alarming rates of spread. New threats of structures in the park headquarters and Far View areas started to come into play. The fire made several additional runs of two to four miles in very short periods of time...During the night, the Park Point Lookout site with the three fire radio caches and the RAWS [Remote Automated Weather Station] were burnt over...The fire burned approximately 10,000 acres during this period.

FIRE BEHAVIOR

...The fire behavior on this fire was extreme/advanced rapidly transitioning to plume dominated conditions. These conditions were witnessed on four consecutive days, July 21, 2000, to July 24, 2000, and seemed to be the norm rather than the exception... because plume dominated or fuel driven fires do not readily lend themselves to modeling predictions, the team was unable to determine any pattern or advanced spread calculations.

– **Excerpts from Incident Management Team reports**

fighters were so eager for the "excitement" of a big fire that they didn't put this one out right away, but rather let it burn so they could work on it for several days. Nothing could have been further from the truth. Firefighters are highly trained; they care deeply about safety; and they follow the rules. Many personally knew a firefighter who died in the line of duty. Fatal errors that have cost lives in the past almost always had an element of trying to fight the fire too aggressively without enough information or manpower. Poor communication can cost lives. That is why firefighters are adamant about having an action plan in place that everyone understands before "engaging" the fire.

... THE BIRCHER FIRE WAS ONE OF THE MOST UNPREDICTABLE, DANGEROUS FIRES MANY VETERAN FIREFIGHTERS HAD EVER SEEN.

Firefighters have been seriously injured and often disabled simply because they didn't have the proper equipment. Without the right gloves and fire-resistant clothing, firefighters have been horribly burned. With no shelter or training on how to use one, a firefighter trapped in rough terrain is helpless against advancing flames. Appropriate headgear is a must in an environment with so much falling debris. Firefighters, no matter what kind of training they have, simply cannot be allowed on the fire lines without the necessary personal protective equipment.

The first night, flames spread from the valley floor to the top of the ridge along the eastern edge of the park and marched southward well into the night. Over the next several days the Bircher Fire was one of the most unpredictable, dangerous fires many veteran firefighters had ever seen. Relentlessly, it drove first south, then west, back to the north, then west again, continuously shifting direction as it consumed mesa after mesa. Every time the end seemed to be in sight the pattern repeated itself. The large gray mushroom-shaped cloud became a daily fixture in the sky and many wondered if there would be anything left of Mesa Verde before it was all over.

Events were happening so rapidly at the beginning of the Bircher Fire that it was difficult to accurately assess the situation. Park management is responsible for creating a document called the Wildfire Situation Analysis prior to turning the fire over to an incoming team. The analysis provides the new team with valuable information on the potential spread of a fire and the structures at risk. Local managers use their knowledge of terrain, fuels, geography, weather, and drought conditions to make an educated guess about what the incoming team will likely face when they assume control of the fire. During the first full day of the Bircher Fire, Oliverius worked on the analysis, creating and discarding two drafts before finalizing the third attempt. Circumstances were changing so rapidly, the fire quickly outstripped his first two predictions.

"The Bircher Fire was the most efficient fire I've ever been on," Oliverius recalled. "It went against the grain and gobbled up everything in sight!"

Rapidly worsening conditions prompted a second change in management less than

News trucks are a daily fixture during the height of any park fire, but especially the Bircher Fire, which was the biggest media event of all. It was the largest fire in the state of Colorado up to that point.

two days later. Hartman's team – known as a Type II IMT – was a regional resource and fully qualified to manage large fires. But the Bircher Fire wasn't *just* a large fire. It was turning into a complex and controversial one. In addition to its extreme fire behavior and potential to spread significantly, it overlapped into multiple jurisdictions, forced the evacuation of thousands of park visitors, as well as employees and ultimately park residents, threatened several private and government structures, and shut down one of the region's main economic anchors during the busiest time of the year. By the end of the second day, Hartman and his team recommended that park officials order a Type I IMT. Type I teams are national resources that are generally called in to manage large fires with many complicating factors

The Type I team came from the Pacific Northwest, headed by Mike Lohrey. They took command on Tuesday, July 25, at 6 a.m.

The team's public information officer, Justin Dombrowski, had his hands full with the media. Interest in the Bircher Fire was intense and came from as far away as Great Britain. Stories about the fire at Mesa Verde National Park appeared on CNN, NBC, ABC, CBS, NPR, and "Good Morning America" as well as in the *Denver Post*, the *Washington Post*, and many others. There were four to nine satellite trucks at the Incident Command Post daily and the competition between reporters and photographers was vigorous. A Bircher Fire website received about 2,000 hits per day at the peak of operations, and more than 23,000 hits in total. Most of the media coverage dealt positively with the balance between protecting archaeological sites and firefighting, but the fire's impact on surrounding commu-

View from the east escarpment.

nities didn't get as much attention. Many area businesses rely almost entirely on tourism for their livelihood. Closure of the park for 23 of what are normally the 30 busiest days of the year was devastating for many small businesses.

At the start of the Bircher Fire, adrenaline kept most everyone going through the initial 16-plus-hour days. As the days turned into a week or more, the lack of sleep started to wear on people. Tempers flared and tears began to flow.

Finally, 11 days after the evacuation of Mesa Verde National Park, on July 31, firefighters declared the Bircher Fire 100 percent contained. It had encompassed 23,607 acres. But containment did not signal the end of danger, because the conditions that spawned the fire remained. As park residents returned to their homes and employees to their jobs, officials warned of continuing fire danger in southwestern Colorado.

The next day, those warnings echoed in everyone's minds as yet another in a long series of dry thunderstorms passed over the Mesa Verde area. The following afternoon, August 2, low relative humidity, low fuel moistures, and excessive fuel loads combined with a smoldering lightning strike to spark the Pony Fire. As before, the fire began outside the park, this time on Ute Mountain Ute tribal land. But once again it headed for Mesa Verde.

Plans had been in the works all week to reopen the national park after its 15-day closure. With the Pony Fire actively burning and highly visible, Mesa Verde opened its doors on Friday, August 4, for day use only. As the last visitors were carefully escorted out of the park at 6 p.m., the Mesa Verde senior management team

Vince Macmillan, Jim Hampson, Laura Martin and Paul Bohman assessing immediate fire effects to archaeological sites.

met with Superintendent Wiese. They assessed the situation and made plans to move all residents out of the park in a calm, orderly evacuation Sunday morning.

Firefighters knew what *should* happen. As the sun sets, relative humidity rises and fires "lie down" for the night. But so far, nothing during the summer of 2000 had gone the way it was predicted. Fed by swirling winds and extreme conditions, the Pony Fire blew up Friday night. By 9 p.m. Superintendent Wiese directed park residents to evacuate for the second time in just over two weeks.

Employees and their families hurriedly repacked their most important belongings as the fire raced across Wetherill Mesa, just two canyons away from their homes. People in nearby Cortez and Mancos watched the sky glow bright red over Wetherill Mesa until well past 2 a.m. The nightmare was starting again.

Dave Sisk's Type II Incident Management Team was just completing their assignment on the Cabezon Fire on the Southern Ute Reservation west of Pagosa Springs when they were alerted they might be reassigned to a new fire at Mesa Verde. The Team was staged in Cortez and assumed command of the Pony Fire the next day, August 5.

An all-day air assault with air tankers and helicopters helped slow the fire's rapid spread. In the daytime, swirling winds caused by the downdrafts of a plume-dominated fire created the most erratic behavior of all, making it impossible to predict what direction it would turn. Given the nature of the drought-stricken vegetation, the night-time fire behavior was spectacular as well. Without enough

Mesa Verde National Park

The eerie sky during the day wore on peoples' nerves. It was a constant reminder of the battle they were fighting. It was easy to lose track of time, because the light during the day always looks the same.

humidity at night to quell the fire, flames approaching 100 feet and higher licked the night sky, creating the illusion of a huge city on the horizon with nothing but red lights glowing through fog until early morning. Lit from within by a huge, orange-red light, the strange cloud looked ominous. Because of the fire's impact on local communities, the fact that it started outside the park, and the second evacuation of the park within a week, Lohrey's Type I team was re-ordered and arrived late on Sunday, August 6.

While substantially smaller than the Bircher Fire, the 5,100-acre Pony Fire was ultimately the more dangerous to the park's infrastructure and cultural resources.

It burned to within two miles of the Mesa Verde Research Center on Chapin Mesa, home to a three-million-object collection of archaeological treasures and archives. It marched across the developed area of Wetherill Mesa, burning all of the modern structures. Only the metal roof and support beams remained of a pavilion that had housed a ranger information desk, the Mesa Verde Museum Association bookstore, and the ARAMARK Mesa Verde Company snack bar. A trailer that served as a ranger and first aid station was incinerated. Strong fire-spawned winds ripped roof panels from the building, blowing them a quarter-mile away. The comfort station was nearly unrecognizable, with only pipes and sinks remaining, standing at weird angles amid piles of rubble, melted Plexiglas, and shredded fiberglass.

With fire, sometimes it's the little things you don't think of that are so striking in the aftermath. The park's maintenance division has a big job taking care of the man-made details.

2

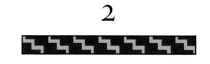

MESA VERDE NATIONAL PARK
FIRE HISTORY

Chapin 5 Fire headed toward Far View Lodge and the Far View Visitor Center.

P rior to the Bircher Fire, the largest recorded fire since the establishment of Mesa Verde National Park in 1906 was the 1996 Chapin 5 Fire, at 4,781 acres. Before that, the Long Mesa '89 Fire measured 2,400 acres. All-out fire suppression came into practice in the 1930s, during the time of the Civilian Conservation Corps. The practice of putting out every fire on park land over the course of seven decades has contributed, at least in part, to an increasingly volatile situation. Combined with extreme weather conditions, those factors culminated in the catastrophic fires in the summer of 2000.

The recorded fire history at Mesa Verde National Park began in 1926. Through the summer of 2003 there were 11 fires in the park that measured at least 200 acres. Of the nearly 750 recorded fires, slightly more than 1 percent were large enough to require an incident management team. The majority of fires in the park are one-tenth of an acre – the smallest unit of measurement described in fire reporting – and typically involve a single tree. Of all fires recorded in the park, approximately 0.6 percent are caused by people, most often involving smoking or campfires.

Lightning causes more than 99 percent of the fires at Mesa Verde. In the United States, only Florida experiences more lightning strikes than the Four Corners area. The high, sloping hills – or cuestas – of Mesa Verde are especially susceptible during the monsoon season in July and August. Mesa Verde's promi-nence high above the surrounding landscape makes it something of a lightning rod, experiencing thousands of strikes in the course of the summer. Hot summer

Above: Chapin 5 Fire coming up the canyon August 19, 1996. The fire gathered strength, speed, and intensity as it ran up-canyon and up-slope. Below: The flame front is visible across the entire canyon, later that same day. The orange glow in the smoke, hundreds of feet above the ground illustrates the intensity of this fire – it was extremely hot with impressive flame lengths at this point.

months are prone to afternoon thunderstorms which produce very little rain in this high, arid desert environment. Lightning usually strikes in the late afternoon and evening, and a stricken tree may smolder overnight or even for days.

In the day following a thunderstorm, during the heat of the afternoon the fire lookout on duty at Park Point can spot a half dozen or more "smokes." Park policy, which is currently under revision in 2005, has dictated that these small fires must be extinguished quickly whenever possible to prevent damage to Mesa Verde's rich archaeological treasures. Unfortunately, under especially hot and dry conditions, these small fires can defy even the best efforts to put them out. As former Chief Ranger Charlie Peterson says, "at Mesa Verde we either burn one tree or one mesa." There doesn't seem to be any middle ground.

Large fires are devastating in many ways. Park employees and their families are displaced. Tourists are unwilling or unable to visit the park, which in turn causes businesses in surrounding communities to lose money. Archaeological sites often suffer fire damage, followed by the effects of post-fire erosion. And sadly, the ecosystem and its many inhabitants are often the hardest hit. Animals are often unable to escape a rapidly advancing fire and those that do still face destroyed habitat. Some of the few small stands of centuries-old trees are lost as well. With so many negative effects, it is easy to overlook the important fact that fire is a natural occurrence and there is much to be learned and gained from wildland fire.

President Franklin Delano Roosevelt's Civilian Conservation Corps (the CCC) was hard at work in Mesa Verde National Park in 1934 when the Wild Horse Mesa and Wickiup Mesa fires began within two days of each other and combined to burn in excess of 4,400 acres. The Wild Horse Mesa Fire, which began July 9 and burned 4,206 acres, actually started on Ute Mountain Ute land and wasn't spotted right away. The Wickiup Mesa Fire started on July 11 and consumed 286 acres before it burned into the Wild Horse Mesa Fire. With no roads to Wetherill

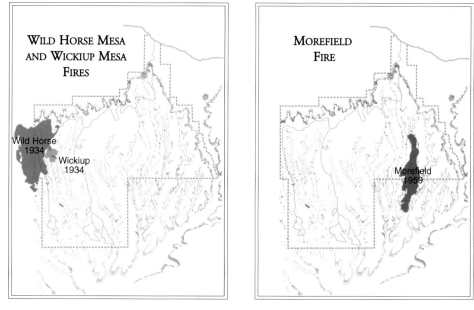

WILD HORSE MESA
AND WICKIUP MESA
FIRES

Wild Horse
1934

Wickiup
1934

MOREFIELD
FIRE

Morefield
1959

Mesa at the time, getting to that remote section of the park was both difficult and time-consuming. Thirteen hundred CCC enrollees bulldozed the first road out to Wetherill that summer. The fires also prompted park officials to acknowledge the need for lookout towers and fire roads in the park. The CCC finished the tower at Park Point, the highest point in the park at 8,571 feet, in 1940. It was first staffed the summer of 1941. The second permanent lookout was established in 1944 at Cedar Tree Tower, near park headquarters.

A mid-summer fire in 1959 prompted several changes in the national park's fire management. On July 18, the Morefield Fire began on Whites Mesa, one of the few places not visible from Park Point, and grew to nearly 2,500 acres before it was contained. Inadequate access to remote parts of the park and insufficient lookouts were again identified as obstacles to fire suppression at Mesa Verde. The Whites Mesa lookout tower and cabin were built in 1960. Forty years later, the cabin was lost in the Bircher Fire. As a result of the 1959 fire, the park service also purchased its first slip-on pumper – a small self-contained water tank and pump that can be slipped into the bed of a pickup truck – and hired its first two firefighters. The fire program at Mesa Verde was underway.

The year 1965 was only the third without fire in Mesa Verde's then 59-year history. Under a new cooperative agreement signed in 1963, the Bureau of Land Management assisted with fire suppression by patrolling the park from the air following thunderstorms. Only three flights were required in 1965, costing the park a total of $21. Park officials agreed the price of $7 per flight was well worth the added ability to detect fires quickly. In addition, the U.S. Forest Service now had the ability to install a temporary slurry reloading base in Durango when a serious fire erupted in the zone. From there, slurry bombers were able to drop fire retardant anywhere in the park with a turnaround time of less than 45 minutes, a substantial improvement over the days when the planes had to make a two-and-one-half-hour round trip to Albuquerque or Grand Junction to reload.

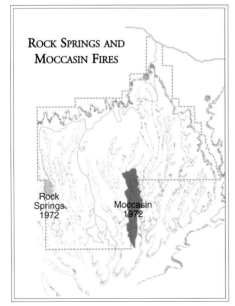

ROCK SPRINGS AND
MOCCASIN FIRES

Rock
Springs
1972

Moccasin
1972

Seven years later, 1972 became a pivotal year in the history of firefighting at Mesa Verde. Up to then, park employees had full-time jobs and fought fire when the need arose, on put-together teams. The 700-acre Rock Springs Fire and the Moccasin Mesa Fire, at 2,680 acres, convinced management that their response time was too slow. The park needed a helicopter, but that was more easily said than done. An operations base would be needed, with agency supervision and a helicopter crew. There seemed no way to justify the expense outside of fire season, especially for a relatively small park like Mesa Verde. Initially, the park used a call-when-needed contract helicopter based in Durango.

In 1979, the first interagency agree-

Spalling rock damage done by the Chapin Fire at a site in Soda Canyon. Notice the pink spots on black. Post-fire erosion is the greatest threat to archaeological sites.

ment provided for a government helicopter at Mesa Verde National Park during fire season, and the Chapin Helibase was constructed. Throughout the 1980s, the National Park Service, Bureau of Indian Affairs, and Bureau of Land Management participated in an interagency agreement which allowed for exclusive use of the helicopter based at Mesa Verde. In various combinations, federal land management agencies – including the U.S. Forest Service and Bureau of Reclamation – contributed to the cost and utilized the helicopter until 2001. These days, a helibase for four months during the summer can cost from $500,000 to $1 million and beyond in a busy fire year, so in 2002 Mesa Verde went back to using a private helicopter under an interagency contract for exclusive use. Most recently, the helibase has been moved out of the park to Fort Lewis, an old army base and school located 15 miles east of the park. Without the amenities necessary for a permanent helibase in the park, the Fort Lewis location provides a low-cost alternative that assures quick response time for all participating agencies.

"With the helicopter we got good at putting out fires," Oliverius recalled.

There was another significant outcome of the fires in 1972. Until that time bulldozers were used without much thought given to the archaeological resources in the park. During the Moccasin Mesa Fire that year, bulldozers cut a swath up to six blade lengths wide in some areas, destroying large pueblo sites. The fire never reached many of these lines and the scars still exist today as testimony to the lack of awareness or concern about damage to Mesa Verde's irreplaceable cultural resources.

As a result, national standards were established that required archaeologists to be on the line with firefighters whenever cultural resources were involved. The park has experienced six large fires since this time, but fire suppression efforts have inflicted relatively little damage to archaeological sites.

The Long Mesa '89 Fire prompted park officials to take a close look at fire history in Mesa Verde. Up to that point, employees serving as part-time firefighters had on-the-ground experience. But they did not fully understand the whole burn cycle of a large pinyon-juniper forest, why the "fuel loading" was so high and just how dangerous it was going to be if and when a fire finally got started and took off. Mesa Verde National Park hired Dr. Bill Romme from Fort Lewis College and Dr. Lisa Floyd-Hanna from Prescott College to research and write a history of fire and post-fire effects. In addition, the regional office of the National Park Service conducted a detailed review of the firefighting operation on the Long Mesa '89 Fire. The professors' report affirmed Mesa Verde's importance as home to one of the largest collections of cultural resources in the world. Both park and regional office staff recognized the disastrous potential of a large fire on Chapin Mesa, an area with a large concentration of important cultural resources. The review team recommended a detailed fire readiness plan for Chapin Mesa that included establishment of pre-determined lines of defense, tree thinning around developments, structural protection planning including availability of water for firefighting, pre-determined priorities for protection of structures and cultural resources, alternative evacuation plans and routes, and potential for low intensity prescribed burning.

Although the federal government had been planning a national fire program, it took the devastating fires in Yellowstone National Park in 1988 and the Long Mesa '89 Fire in Mesa Verde to compel full implementation of the program. After that time, funding increased significantly for fire programs across the country.

The National Interagency Fire Center (NIFC) in Boise, Idaho, now coordinates all federal interagency firefighting efforts. A multitude of agencies rely on the center, including the National Park Service, U.S. Forest Service, Bureau of Land Management, Fish and Wildlife Service, National Oceanic & Atmospheric Administration, Office of Aircraft Services, National Association of State Foresters, and Bureau of Indian Affairs. They work cooperatively to coordinate and mobilize funding, equipment, aircraft, fire crews, and overhead personnel for all firefighting efforts on public lands. The interagency dispatch center is one of the benefits of this system. NIFC is able to search its enormous database of all the firefighting resources in the country to fill a need without duplication of effort and in the most efficient manner. The command and control center is responsible for prioritizing wildland fires across the country then mobilizing and moving resources throughout the country accordingly.

The need for cooperation doesn't stop with containment or control of a wildland fire. The aftereffects can be as devas-

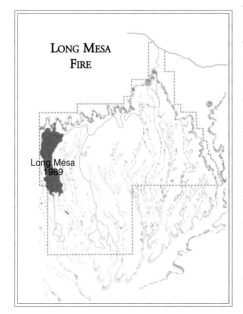

LONG MESA
FIRE

Long Mesa
1989

tating as the fire itself. Anticipating and planning for post-fire problems and rehabilitation of burned areas also became a national concern.

Prior to the Chapin 5 Fire in 1996, each national park was responsible for its own post-fire rehabilitation work. That summer a team from a newly created interagency fire management program came to Mesa Verde. Together with in-house staff experts, the Burned Area Emergency Rehabilitation (BAER) Team assessed damage and recommended strategies for mitigating the most severe consequences of that fire. The Chapin 5 Fire cost $1.5 million to fight and the rehabilitation project cost $1.8 million. Impacts to cultural sites accounted for $1.4 million of that total amount.

Rehabilitation experts start by evaluating the extent of fire damage, then categorizing that damage as low, moderate, or high intensity. The BAER team found that 167 acres of the 4,781 acres attributed to the Chapin 5 Fire were untouched by the fire. Of the remaining land, 882 acres suffered low intensity damage, 2,627 acres moderate intensity, and 1,105 acres high intensity. This information was critical in determining how to prevent additional damage to sites from erosion. The team also documented and assessed fire damage at 668 archaeological sites. Of these, 296 sites were previously recorded from prior surveys and 372 sites were newly recorded sites within the Chapin 5 burn area.

Mesa Verde was one of the first cultural parks served by a BAER team, and while there were certainly bugs to work out of the system, the program was a success. After the Bircher and Pony fires in 2000, the BAER team was not only better equipped to handle the post-fire assessment, but the members also possessed a fair amount of experience to lend credibility to their recommendations.

The 1996 fire season also brought about another positive change for the regional firefighting effort. A national study revealed a gaping hole in the Durango area air tanker service, with no permanent tanker base close enough to effectively serve

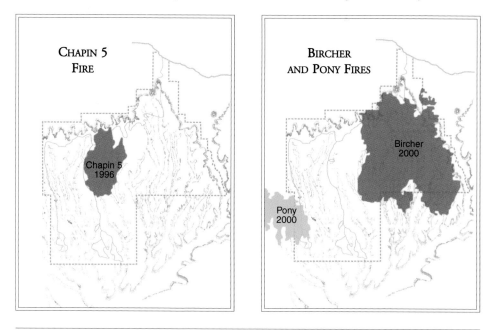

CHAPIN 5
FIRE

Chapin 5
1996

BIRCHER
AND PONY FIRES

Bircher
2000

Pony
2000

the southwestern part of Colorado. Funding was secured, a permanent reload base was established, and planning began for a permanent base with a dedicated staff. Construction began in August 2001 and was completed in July 2002. Firefighters moved into the new facility overnight right in the middle of the Missionary Ridge Fire near Durango.

After the fires of 1996 and 2000 the people in and around Mesa Verde fervently believed the park was due for a break. Nearly half the park's 52,000 acres burned during those two years. Unfortunately, as the drought entered its third year in 2002, it added to the potential for more fires.

Weakened by a severe lack of moisture, pinyon trees fell victim to an infestation of opportunistic Ips bark beetles. Trees that had escaped fire now sickened and died, their green needles turning a pallid brown, then dropping to the parched ground. The pinyons' mortality rate in the remaining forest at Mesa Verde was severe. Faced with extreme fire danger, living trees now were surrounded by beetle-killed pinyons. The forest was a tinder box. It was developing into the driest year in the Southwest in more than three centuries.

By early summer of 2002, fire danger was far worse than it had been in 2000. Officials knew it was only a matter of when, not if, the next fire would strike. All the indicators for extreme fire danger warned of more trouble ahead. Moisture levels in living and dead trees dropped to alarmingly low levels in April and stayed there. The "Energy Release Component," a measurement that analyzes several factors to predict fire danger, did the same. A score above the 88th percentile indicates extreme fire danger in a pinyon-juniper forest. On April 25, it hit the 90th percentile, and stayed at least that high. The 90-day forecast predicted continued hot and dry conditions. Mesa Verde had never experienced such extreme fire danger conditions.

On July 1, Mesa Verde's senior management team decided to restrict access to lower Chapin Mesa, home to the most heavily visited sites in the park. The loop roads leading through dense forest to Cliff Palace, Balcony House, and Spruce Tree House are the farthest point visitors can travel in the park. The thousands who travel those roads daily in the summer would be at greatest risk for becoming trapped by a fire.

On Monday, July 29, park officials' fears were realized. At 2 p.m., a previous day's lightning strike ignited the Long Mesa '02 Fire just north of the developed area on Chapin Mesa. Immediately, rangers drove all the roads, notifying visitors that they needed to head down the hill. The dispatcher called the evacuation order to the rest of the divisions in the park. Employees gathered up important equipment and files while those who lived in the park went to their homes to

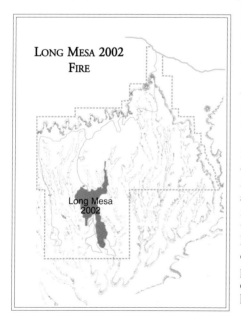

LONG MESA 2002
FIRE

Long Mesa
2002

collect personal belongings. The sight of a black cloud of smoke getting bigger and bigger in such close proximity to the road made it easy to persuade visitors to leave. Approximately 2,000 visitors and employees were evacuated. Amazingly, the bigger problem came in subsequent days, when people arrived to visit the park and were turned away. Some argued that they should be allowed into the park, even with a cloud of smoke in sight.

The fire made significant runs to the south that first night, destroying two employee residences, a sewage treatment plant, the million-gallon water tank, the air quality monitoring station, and power and phone lines. Firefighters working through the night were able to save the majority of the 70-plus structures in the path of the fire, thanks to the decade-long, aggressive "hazardous fuel reduction" program that Tim Oliverius had advocated for so long. It is because of him that the park has made such great strides in thinning, and the aerial photos of the Long Mesa '02 Fire show just how well it has worked.

"WITH FIRES BURNING TO THE EAST AND WEST OF MESA VERDE AND SMOKE FILLING THE AIR FOR WEEKS, THE AWARENESS OF DROUGHT CONDITIONS AND FIRE DANGER REACHED AN ALL-TIME HIGH AMONG PARK EMPLOYEES. "

The Long Mesa '02 Fire burned a total of 2,601 acres in the most developed area of the park. It is a testament to Mesa Verde National Park's highly skilled fire management professionals that only a handful of structures were lost and no one was seriously injured or killed.

Starting in 1982, trees and shrubs were thinned on more than 150 acres to create defensible space in front of cliff dwellings and around historic and modern structures. The distance between trees was widened to 20 feet, reducing the tree and shrub cover by nearly 40 percent. There are still trees with foliage but now people can get a peek through them and tell there are buildings a short distance off the road. This new view farther into the forest bothered some of the residents at first, but it is nothing compared to what can be seen through burned trees which hide nothing. Despite earlier resistance, most residents who thought they didn't want the trees thinned in the first place would gladly take the sparser forest over the burned-out look.

Although the fire burned through some of the treated areas, in most cases the dramatic reduction in fuel slowed the fire's momentum and energy, making it easier to battle. With a less dense canopy of trees, the fire slows, moving out of the treetops onto the ground, where it is much easier to fight. In addition, the retardant dropped by air tankers is able to penetrate all the way to the ground, effectively slowing and stopping the flames in key areas.

Park management had taken several other steps to complement the defensible space around some of the historic structures. They replaced the original wooden shingles on CCC building roofs with composite fire-resistant shingles, and fire crews installed a network of sprinklers on structures as well as on the ground throughout the developed areas during the fire season. They also cleared a 12-acre safety zone near the headquarters, an area that could provide firefighters safe haven from the flames. These measures allowed firefighters to make a successful stand in an area that previously would have been too dangerous, and in turn enabled them to save most of the Chapin Mesa structures.

The Long Mesa '02 Fire in Mesa Verde National Park was not the worst fire in recent park history but it was certainly part of one of the worst fire seasons on record for the state of Colorado. Even before the fire at Mesa Verde, the Hayman Fire near Denver began on June 8 and burned nearly 138,000 acres over the following 25 days, quickly eclipsing the Bircher Fire as the largest fire on record in the state. The Missionary Ridge Fire near Durango was sparked on June 9 that summer and burned 73,391 acres, destroying 83 structures, 56 of which were private homes. Before the fires in Colorado were contained, the Rodeo/Chediski fires in Arizona were ignited, burning a total of 462,614 acres in the east central part of that state; 426 structures were lost.

With fires burning to the east and west of Mesa Verde and smoke filling the air for weeks, the awareness of drought conditions and fire danger reached an all-time high among park employees. The Long Mesa '02 fire began before any of these other fires were contained and it certainly did seem as if the whole state was on fire. When Colorado Governor Bill Owens warned visitors to stay away from the state because of fires, it was the final nail in the coffin of an already dismal tourist season. Although 2000 remained the worst year in Mesa Verde's fire history in terms of acres burned and days lost, 2002 saw 7.2 million acres burned across the country with more than $1 billion expended in firefighting costs – one of the worst fire years nationally in half a century.

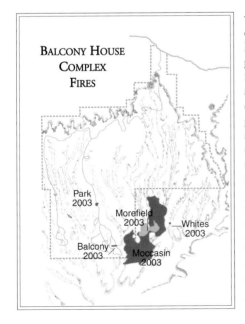

BALCONY HOUSE
COMPLEX
FIRES

Park
2003
Morefield
2003
Whites
2003
Balcony
2003
Moccasin
2003

As bad as 2002 was, 2003 started off worse. Trees, shrubs, and grasses were drying out faster and sooner than they had the previous year. The only saving grace in what looked like another horrible fire season for the park was the locally available firefighting resources. Given the extreme nature of recent years and the grim predictions for the coming fire season, there were a number of helicopter crews, engine crews, and smokejumpers assigned to respond to the first signs of fire in and around Mesa Verde. During periods of extremely high fire danger, firefighters assigned for this initial attack are often staged in strategic areas so that they can respond quickly to new fire starts. They usually work a short time – one or two operational periods – on that fire, then are often quickly reassigned to other new fire starts.

On July 15, 2003, lightning from a late afternoon thunderstorm ignited five fires in the southern part of the park. Once again the threat to major cliff dwellings and developed areas of the park prompted officials to call for an Incident Management Team. Meanwhile, firefighters and equipment already in the area were able to attack the fires quickly, catching the two that were the biggest threats to developed areas before flames could spread. The Type II team from Northern California then took over and managed all five fires in what was deemed the Balcony House Complex.

As with most of the other large fires in Mesa Verde's recent history, the Balcony House Complex had its share of complications. Generally speaking, when it's a bad fire year at Mesa Verde, it is most likely a bad fire year throughout the region, if not the entire western United States. Firefighting resources are stretched thin and are assigned to fires based on regional and national priorities. Because the two fires that most directly threatened park structures were contained early on, it was not until July 19 and 20 that the fires at Mesa Verde were deemed the number one priority in the region and began to get some of the critical resources that had been ordered. However, there were no national Type I hand crews available and air support was in short supply.

When an Incident Management Team is assigned to a large fire they are sometimes also authorized to evaluate new fire starts in the immediate area and make the first efforts to put them out. Frequent thunderstorms are common at Mesa Verde in July and August. Sometimes they arrive with moisture, sometimes without. Storms with dry lightning passed through the area daily in 2003, and on July 17, five crews assigned to the Balcony House Complex were reassigned to mount the initial attack on a new fire before they had even worked their first shift. Such reassignments became a daily event.

The five fires that made up the Balcony House Complex burned a total of 2,730 acres, the majority on Ute Mountain Ute lands. As with so many of the park fires that overlapped boundaries, the steep, rugged terrain made access extremely difficult. Unable to get to some areas of the fires on the ground, firefighters had to rely on assessing them from the air. Surveys using infrared equipment allowed them to determine exactly where the hot spots were. Armed with that information, they could make much more efficient use of resources on the ground, targeting specific areas on which to concentrate their efforts. Considering the severity of the conditions that summer, the fires that made up the Balcony House Complex could have had far more serious consequences than they did. The headquarters area and the loop roads remained the most seriously threatened. But the locations of most of the fires in the complex were well away from developed areas, allowing managers to reopen the park after just five days of closure – a blip on the radar screen compared to previous years.

3

CONDITIONS AT
MESA VERDE

L arge fires have certainly become more frequent at Mesa Verde. Why? With substantial improvements in firefighting techniques and equipment over the past 30 years, it would seem that fires could be contained more quickly and kept in check. The answers lie not in the methods for combating fire, but in the conditions that spawn it.

Increasing "fuel loads" are part of the fire rotation story. Researchers at Mesa Verde believe the pinyon-juniper forest has a natural burn cycle that spans an average of 400 years. These forests grow more and more dense, eventually reaching the point that fire can spread through them easily. It just may be time for a "stand replacement burn" in Mesa Verde's forests.

But a normal fire cycle is only part of the answer. Other factors have played a part in making the forests more susceptible to fire. The large fires that Mesa Verde has experienced, especially since 1989, require a great deal of fuel.

The amount of vegetation per acre, or fuel load, is measured in tons per acre and refers to both live and dead plant material. Pinyon-juniper forests vary widely, but typically have about 20 to 25 tons of burnable vegetation per acre. In Mesa Verde the fuel load is at the upper end of the spectrum for pinyon-juniper forests with almost double that amount, at 35 to 40 tons per acre, most of it trees, including a significant number of dead ones, both standing and fallen.

There are several reasons for these fuel levels, some obvious and some not so obvious. Mesa Verde's history of total fire suppression has certainly played a role in creating the current situation. Over the last 30 years – about the same time that firefighting has developed into a highly specialized field – a policy of putting out every fire has set the stage for a conflagration of Bircher's magnitude. Some fire managers believe that without total suppression Mesa Verde might have experienced three or four more fires in the 3,000- to 5,000-acre range in those decades, but not a 23,200-acre fire.

Mesa Verde's topography is partly responsible for the density of the pinyon-juniper forests. The park's average annual rainfall of 18 inches is at the high end of the scale for this type of forest. Mesa Verde looks flat like a mesa but is actually a series of cuestas – slopes tilting gently to the southwest. The difference is significant because that southwest slope provides more hours of sunlight and therefore longer growing and drying periods than in most of the surrounding areas. In turn, that extended growing season produces a naturally denser forest and more fuel to burn.

The absence of livestock grazing in the park has contributed to the forest's density in a couple of ways. By eating grasses and shrubs among the trees, cattle and sheep kept the undergrowth and therefore ladder fuels in check. Heavy undergrowth provides an avenue for fire to spread from tree to tree. Animals walking through the forest as they grazed – especially cattle – stepped on and killed many of the small shrubs and tree seedlings, thereby maintaining wide spaces between trees. With less ground cover and ladder fuels, and more spacing between trees, lightning fires were more commonly limited to single trees. Over time, with the elimination of grazing in the early 1950s, the ground cover became denser and the shrubs and seedlings had a better chance to survive and give future fires a direct avenue for spreading easily. But livestock alone are not responsible for the build-up of fuels and it is unlikely the park will change its no-grazing policy. Livestock tromping through the backcountry pose too much of a

PLANTS AS FUEL

)f moisture in plant material both living and dead is a key factor in its
ire. Experts have devised a method using the measurement of that
_ predict the likelihood of a fire starting. Moisture levels are first catego-
rized by the size of vegetation and the speed with which it reaches equilibrium with the
relative humidity of the air around it.

Fuel Moisture

Diameter	Time Lag	Examples
0 – ¼"	one-hour fuels	grasses; needles
¼ - 1"	ten-hour fuels	twigs; fuel sticks
1 – 4"	one-hundred-hour fuels	branches
4" & larger	one-thousand-hour fuels	logs; tree trunks

For example, if grasses and needles that are no more than ¼ inch in diameter are
soaked by rain, it takes about an hour after the rain stops for their moisture content to
adjust to the point that it is equal to the moisture content in the air. For twigs and
man-made fuel sticks up to an inch in diameter, it takes about 10 hours.

Larger plants, or parts of plants, are always playing catch-up with the moisture level
of the air around them. They absorb and release moisture slowly, taking as long as
1,000 hours. Relative humidity becomes a moving target, changing too many times in
that span of time for large branches, tree trunks, and logs to ever reach equilibrium. In
a drought, even occasional soaking rains can't increase their moisture content enough to
match that brief spike in relative humidity. They will remain drier than their environment, and quickly lose the brief benefits of occasional rains.

How long rain falls is as important as how much falls. A short downpour will quickly saturate grasses and twigs, but will have less effect on the moisture content of the
larger branches and logs, which need a longer, soaking rain for moisture to penetrate
them. That's why a drought is not over just because it rains once in awhile.

Experts use fuel sticks that simulate 10-hour fuels to determine the moisture in
dead-and-down fuels. They weigh the sticks, then place them out in the environment
where they absorb moisture from the surrounding atmosphere for 24 hours. The sticks
are then re-weighed to determine their moisture content.

Leaves and pine needles are used to determine live fuel moistures. Experts weigh
them before and after heating them in a special oven for 24 hours at 212 degrees
Fahrenheit. The difference between their weight before and after their trip to the oven
is expressed as a percentage of moisture.

Moisture levels are different for each tree species. The final step, then, is to consult a
chart and determine how the laboratory findings compare to normal moisture levels in
particular species. The farther below normal moisture levels, the greater the likelihood a
fire will start in that type of forest.

Moisture levels in living trees have more influence on whether a forest undergoes a
severe stand-replacing wildfire than does dead fuel moisture. The most important factor
for live trees is the amount of winter moisture that fell, penetrated deep into the soil
and remains available to the trees during the growing season.

threat to delicate archaeological sites.

Through the centuries of their natural burn cycle, pinyon-juniper forests grow increasingly dense because the forest will only burn under very specific environmental conditions. Unless those conditions exist, fire is frequently confined to a single tree. As many as 50 such fires occur within the park each summer, and another 40 to 50 on land surrounding the park.

Aside from the density of the forests, below-average precipitation also contributes to increased fire danger. The fire management staff tracks precipitation on a 12-month basis from October through the following September. October 1, 1999, was the beginning of one of the driest years on record in southwestern Colorado. Through August 2000, precipitation was 63 percent of normal.

By itself, though, low rainfall wasn't enough to account for conditions that summer. Relative humidity, temperatures, fuel types and moisture levels in living and dead plant materials all played a role. A measurement of those factors yields a rating which is far more accurate than precipitation alone in predicting fire danger during long-term drought. The Energy Release Component Level, or ERC, rates each plant community – or fuel type – differently. Mesa Verde's pinyon-juniper forest is considered to be under extreme fire danger when the ERC rating is 88 or higher. Prior to the Bircher Fire, ERC levels exceeded 100 for several weeks. The levels were even higher in 2002 and 2003.

Fuel-moisture level is one of the most critical parts of the ERC equation. Fire management personnel measure the moisture level in both living and dead plants, expressing it as a percentage of the plant's dry weight. In late June and early July 2000, the moisture level in dead logs that were at least four inches in diameter and lying on the ground ranged from 6 percent to 7 percent. Those levels were lower than kiln-dried wood – drier than the boards in a lumberyard.

Every week during fire season someone from the fire management office reviews all the numbers from the previous week at a Monday morning park senior management team meeting. The information is critical to planning efforts for the upcoming week. The primary concern is for visitor safety, mitigating the danger as much as possible without restricting visitor services unless absolutely necessary. This includes tree thinning, cutting a safety zone, having a current evacuation plan, having the most current information at hand, and having a well-trained fire crew.

4

FIRE BEHAVIOR

Looking at Point Lookout from the northeast of the Mesa Verde Park entrance, during the Bircher Fire. This was a day when it seemed like the entire park was on fire.

 lthough a pinyon-juniper forest may be relatively difficult to burn under normal circumstances, once a fire begins in this environment during a drought, it is also very difficult to stop.

Three factors determine how a fire will behave: weather, fuel, and terrain. Under the right conditions – low relative humidity and fuel moistures coupled with high winds and temperatures – a single tree fire can easily begin running along the ground. The fire may quickly consume grass, brush, and small trees, using them as ladder fuels to climb into mature trees. Once in the trees, it can become a crown fire and advance through the canopy or tree-tops of a forest instead of along the ground. Once a crown fire begins to gather strength and momentum, under certain conditions it may become a plume-dominated fire. Such intense fires send columns of smoke 10,000 to 40,000 feet into the air.

The Bircher Fire sent a column of smoke 56,000 feet into the atmosphere, according to the National Weather Service.

Often described as mushroom clouds, these smoke columns are commonly referred to as pyro-cumulus. When a fire reaches these proportions, it truly takes on a life of its own. It begins to create its own weather, including downdrafts and winds swirling and blowing in every direction, making it impossible to predict what direction the fire will go. Plume-dominated fires can be characterized by incredibly destructive firestorms, with huge rolling balls of flame up to 200 to 300 feet in height. The awesome sight of such fires is a sobering reminder of man's powerlessness against such forces of nature. It also becomes very clear why little

Mesa Verde National Park

Bircher Fire air support reinforcing a natural fire line created by a change in fuel type. This is where the Bircher Fire met the Chapin 5 Fire.

Crews during the Bircher Fire reinforcing the same fire line, making sure there was a line all the way around the fire perimeter.

can be done to control such fires until there are significant changes in the fuels, weather, or terrain.

Scott McDermid is a helicopter manager who handles initial attack on fires. Usually one of the first on the scene on big fires in Mesa Verde, McDermid said what he saw in 2000 was "unprecedented fire behavior for this area that was the culmination of heavy fuel loading and prolonged drought."

Firefighters will say they do not put out fire, they fight fire. They attempt to contain and then gain control of large fires.

They first create an anchor point, generally near the point of ignition, and from there begin to flank the fire by clearing all vegetation down to bare soil on a swath of ground along the sides, then moving toward the head of the fire. When conditions are right, they close the fire line to achieve containment, an achievement they refer to as "pinching it off." Containment is unlikely unless at least one of the three factors changes. Fuel can run out, giving the fire nothing to feed on. The weather can change bringing lower winds, lower temperatures, higher relative humidity, or rain. Or the terrain can change to one less conducive to the spread of fire. Generally, it is some combination of these factors that enables firefighters to gain the upper hand. In 1996, the Chapin 5 Fire ran uncontrolled for three days up-slope and up-canyon with southwest winds pushing it along. About the time the fire reached the north escarpment of the park where the terrain is a sheer rocky cliff rather than a fuel-laden slope, the relative humidity rose and the rains came.

Weather is obviously the most unpredictable of the three elements that dictate fire behavior. In southwestern Colorado the prevailing winds are generally out of the south-southwest. With the help of National Weather Service information, it is

Mesa Verde National Park

**Scott McDermid takes a much needed breather at the end of a long
day of battling the blaze.**

One of the many places the Bircher Fire jumped the road, in Prater Canyon. It's easy to see that the road isn't much of a firebreak to a fast-moving, intense fire, especially one moving uphill. The wooden posts supporting the guardrails are quickly devoured by flames dropping the metal rails to the ground.

typically possible to predict weather patterns or trends. During the Bircher and Pony fires, however, very uncharacteristic winds blowing from every direction produced some of the most erratic fire behavior ever observed in the region.

Relative humidity – the water vapor content of air at a given temperature – also played a tremendous role during the summer of 2000. Typically, humidity drops during the day, creating a peak burning period from about 10 a.m. to 6 p.m. During the night, temperature falls and relative humidity increases, causing a fire to "lie down." For this reason firefighters are usually up before dawn, attending briefings, and heading out to the line, hoping to get a jump on a fire before the day heats up. Once again, the Bircher and Pony fires didn't behave according to the norm. Firefighters generally hope for relative humidity to climb to 40 percent or higher overnight. During the Bircher and Pony fires, it rarely exceeded 20 percent. Local residents could look out their windows at 2 a.m. and see active flames – something that just isn't supposed to happen.

"I looked over at Whites Mesa at about 11 p.m. and I saw an active flame front that must have been nearly five miles long," Tim Oliverius recalled. "Then I looked again at 5:30 a.m. and it was still actively burning."

5

PARK SERVICE
FIRE MANAGEMENT POLICY

Mesa Verde is bound by the laws, regulations, and national policies that govern the National Park Service, as well as by the concerns and interests of visitors. Fire management policy at Mesa Verde has been, and continues to be, dictated by the need to put out all wildfires.

Fire suppression is aimed at saving more than trees and wildlife. It protects archaeological resources as well as human life. Mesa Verde's single road into and out of the park increases the danger of employees and visitors becoming trapped. Awareness of that risk has prompted park officials to always err on the side of caution when making decisions about evacuating or closing the park.

Of the available methods park managers can use to combat or prevent wildfires, they use suppression, prescribed burns, and "mechanical fuel removal," or thinning of trees and shrubs. Suppression, the aggressive fighting of any fire that starts within park boundaries, has been the basic approach to wildfires throughout the United States since early in the 20th century.

"FIRE SUPPRESSION IS AIMED AT SAVING MORE THAN TREES
AND WILDLIFE. IT PROTECTS ARCHAEOLOGICAL RESOURCES
AS WELL AS HUMAN LIFE. "

The fire lookout tower at Park Point is staffed throughout the summer and any time of the year when fire danger is serious enough to warrant special vigilance. The ranger on duty constantly scans the horizon for developing thunderstorms, lightning strikes, or "smokes" that indicate a new fire. Equipped with maps and locating equipment, the ranger can pinpoint the exact location of a fire and report it to the park radio dispatch center.

A tree hit by lightning sometimes smolders undetected for several days. When the tree begins to burn actively, it produces more smoke which is often visible for miles through the park's clear air and long vistas. It is not unusual to spot several smokes at one time on a hot and dry summer day. A helicopter and helitack crew are on standby to monitor the situation from the air. Should the situation become more serious, they will drop a crew of firefighters into the field to assess the situation on the ground and try to fight the fire, then return to drop buckets of water on the fire. Most of the time, that is all that is needed to contain and control the burn.

The most important resources on a wildland fire are the helicopters and air tankers. Fire crews cannot safely make a direct attack on fires when flames are higher than four feet. Mechanical equipment – engines and dozers – can safely work on a fire with up to eight-foot flames. When faced with 50- to 100-foot flames, air operations are often the only reasonably safe course of action. Helicopters with a long line and a bucket are able to scoop water or retardant from dip tanks to drop on the fire. In reality, though, even air tankers and helicopters are no match for flame lengths much over 12 feet. At that point, their role is to stem the spread of fire by pre-treating available fuels ahead of the fire. Air tankers of varying size are able to deliver from 400 to 3,500 gallons of retardant in

Sprinklers have been set up around buildings, as firefighters rendezvous in a safety zone and prepare to defend Morefield Campground from approaching fire.

a single load.

During the last days of the Bircher Fire as flames approached Park Point, firefighters saw an opportunity to significantly reinforce the fire line. The boundary of the 1996 Chapin 5 Fire, where vegetation was both small and sparse, offered a break in the dense shrubland being consumed by the fire. Six air tankers began laying down a line of retardant along the edge of the old burn area. The combination of a significant reduction in fuel and fire retardant helped stop the fire's advance. Dyed red so that pilots can see previous drops and make a continuous line, retardant is chemically very similar to fertilizer. It reacts with vegetation to create an environment that is not conducive to fire, lowering the combustibility of whatever it coats. Retardant cannot extinguish flames, but used in this way, it is very effective as an enhancement to a natural firebreak.

Air operations for firefighting require precise coordination. In an air attack, one plane usually circles over the fire, directing and coordinating all operations. In addition, a lead plane scouts out the best path for tankers to follow when making their drops, checking for turbulence and up- or down-drafts. The lead plane is also responsible for clearing the fire line of personnel prior to the retardant drop. First the lead plane flies the route alone. Then the air tanker flies a dry run, and on a final pass it drops the retardant.

Prescribed burning is a recent approach to fire prevention that uses deliberately set fire under very strict conditions to reduce the fuel load and lessen the probability of a large, destructive wildfire. The prescribed fire program at Mesa Verde began in October 1999, when two small controlled burns of 12 and 13 acres were

Mesa Verde National Park

Once an active flame front has passed, helicopters are very effective on hot spots like this. This is a Skycrane.

Mesa Verde National Park

Mesa Verde National Park

Bombers laid down line after line of fire retardant in their successful attempt to save Far View Visitor Center and Lodge during the Chapin 5 Fire.

A perfect illustration of how tree thinning and retardant lines can work together to save valuable archaeological sites.

successfully carried out in the Far View area. Computer models assist the fire manager in creating a set of parameters that must exist before the fire is set. At Mesa Verde, a fairly narrow range of temperature, wind, relative humidity, and fuel moisture conditions must be met before a prescribed burn is allowed to proceed. The state of Colorado must give permission and local government agencies must be notified before a burn is ignited.

Pinyon and juniper trees are not as fire resistant as other larger evergreen species such as ponderosa pine. A prescribed burn designed to clear out the underbrush and dead material on the ground has a good chance of killing an unacceptably high number of trees in pinyon-juniper forest. There are, however, techniques that can be used to set very slow-moving ground fires, taking care to keep the trees from being scorched.

Ground crews may cut down trees and brush, and in some instances remove the wood, to reduce fire risk. Mesa Verde solicits bids on the wood that is useful for firewood and sets a deadline for the winning bidder to remove it from the park. The remaining slash – the branches left over after the usable firewood is removed – is gathered into a large pile which Mesa Verde firefighters burn when the danger of the fire spreading is remote, usually in late fall or early winter. In an area with high density of archaeological sites like Mesa Verde, such thinning may be preferable to prescribed fire. Although it may be more costly and less efficient than prescribed fire, the effects of chain saws can be more easily and precisely controlled. Mesa Verde has used this approach since 1993 to thin the pinyon-juniper forests along the park road between Far View and the headquarters area, the areas surrounding the park housing complexes, historic park offices, and visitor facilities on Chapin Mesa. When the Bircher and Pony fires were burning in the summer of 2000, chain saw crews created safe zones and firebreaks.

The first rule of firefighting is to keep people safe and one of the best ways to do that is to keep the fire on the ground. Ideally, prescribed burns would be used in concert with thinning to accomplish that goal. With trees properly spaced through thinning, prescribed burning can be used to eliminate the ladder fuel grasses and shrubs that carry fire up into tree branches and the canopy.

Thinning of trees and shrubs at Mesa Verde has provoked some controversy in recent years. National parks are set aside to preserve and protect natural and cultural resources. Cutting down trees appears to contradict that policy. Perhaps because the Chapin 5 Fire hit so close to home, thinning of trees and shrubs was more readily accepted during the next few years. The benefits were evident when, during the summer of 2002, firefighters believed the trees and brush had been thinned enough to warrant an effort to protect structures in the headquarters area. Even so, firefighters would not have been sent into that area without safe zones nearby. Only then would the incident commander allow people to stay in the area to defend the structures.

6

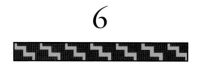

POST-FIRE
ARCHAEOLOGY

Mug House on Wetherill Mesa after the Pony Fire in 2000.
All vegetation burned, leaving cultural deposits vulnerable to washing down the slope.

I t will take decades to fully assess what the fires have done to Mesa Verde's cultural and natural resources. In broad terms, the effects are twofold, including not only the impact of the fires themselves but also the longer range aftereffects. The savage intensity of wildfires destroyed almost everything in their path. Weeks later, when the ashes cooled, and the landscape had been stripped of much of its dense vegetation, the destructive power of erosion posed a serious threat.

Smoke and flames inflicted some direct damage to archaeological sites. At several sites, heat fractured building stones and caused wall stones and petroglyph panels to peel away in layers. This spalling also damaged rocks that had been used for tool-making. The heat from a tree burning next to Cedar Tree Tower caused some oxidation and spalling of the building's stones. Intense heat damaged artifacts as well, burning structural wood and causing oxidation and soot damage to potsherds. Anything that is organic is lost if it comes in direct contact with fire. Artifacts lying on the surface may suffer oxidation and sooting damage. However, because most artifacts are buried and fire only penetrates a few centimeters below the topsoil, many are spared direct fire damage.

Occasionally pack rat middens, which are loose collections of sticks, leaves, and feces these rodents leave in crevices within archaeological sites, ignited. One such fire, in Mushroom House, burned for three days after the Pony Fire moved through the site. The smoldering fire sooted and spalled building stones and caused mortar in the wall joints to break. The fires often burned trees down through their roots, leaving the ground pockmarked with craters. Such craters pose a special danger when they are close to prehistoric walls, where they can under-

Fire damages remnants on the ground's surface. The upper left corner of this pottery sherd shows spalling, the outer layer of it is gone. The rest of the sherd is blackened and oxidized.

mine the building stones and cause the structures to collapse.

Firefighting efforts inflicted some damage as well, including some slurry staining above Spruce Tree House and on the historic structures at Spruce Tree Terrace. After the fires had cooled, erosion had a severe impact on farming terraces near Cedar Tree Tower. Ancestral Puebloans designed the terraces to slow water runoff and trap dirt behind them for farming plots. But with no vegetation in the surrounding area, the higher than normal runoff was too much for the check dams to handle. There is a litany of potential negative effects from post-fire erosion including: artifacts being displaced, burials eroding, standing architecture collapsing, and trees uprooting architecture. In a downpour, hundreds of small rivulets come together in drainages to produce flash floods, greatly increasing the water's destructive potential. Often more so than direct fire damage, these are the types of issues that most concern archaeologists. Erosion's power to destroy archaeological resources cannot be overstated.

With just over 21,000 acres of park land affected by the twin wildfires of 2000, archaeologists had a huge area of backcountry to study and assess. That autumn, field crews spent seven weeks working in Morefield and Prater canyons, just off the park road. In subsequent field seasons, they worked in areas that were much more difficult to reach. Sometimes helicopters dropped crews onto mesas in the remote southern section of the park, and sometimes the location of sites required crews to hike for hours through the hot, dry, dusty backcountry to reach the burn area. In some cases "spike camps," temporary base camps in remote areas, allowed crews to spend more time assessing and treating the archaeological sites and less time in transit.

Typically, these crews start with sketch maps of known archaeological sites, which in Mesa Verde might be kivas, towers, single pueblo structures, room blocks, cliff dwellings or other archaeological features in alcoves, and farming sites. Archaeologists record the site and its features, create a map, document direct and

As fire passes and smoke clears, this is the kind of sight sometimes encountered by archaeologists as they survey burned areas. This is the rubble mound from a surface site – there were several previously unrecorded sites in this area, their remnants hidden by dense overgrowth.

indirect fire effects and photograph the site and its condition. They then make recommendations for specific treatments to help slow the effects of erosion.

Two of the most visible examples of post-fire damage are in Fewkes Canyon, which was burned in the Long Mesa '02 Fire. Fire Temple and Oak Tree House suffered some damage from immediate post-fire erosion and subsequent waterfalls pouring off the cliff edge. Excelsior logs and log diverters, placed above the alcoves within days of the fire, have been very effective in diverting runoff. The crews also treated Spruce Tree House just to be sure there would be no damage from runoff even though there was some vegetation left above that site.

Hemenway House was first thought to have suffered severe damage from runoff. A black waterfall was observed pouring off the cliff above the site in September 2003 following the Balcony House Complex Fires. It was thought that the water was hitting standing walls in the cliff dwelling Once in the site, however, crews were grateful to learn that the damage was minimal. Following the 1996 Chapin 5 Fire, walls in the alcoves of two Soda Canyon sites, 5mv541 and 5mv542, were covered with mud and ash from runoff above the sites. The Balcony House Complex fire caused similar problems to another Soda Canyon site, 5mv3758. Previous erosion problems are often exacerbated after a fire. Located in a natural "pour-off," the walls of the Soda Canyon site were completely covered with soot and mud. Crews cleaned the walls during the summer of 2004 and it happened again immediately after the next rain.

These protection techniques, for the most part, were developed in the aftermath of the Dome Fire at Bandelier National Monument and Chapin 5 Fire at Mesa Verde in 1996, and further refined in the wake of the summer of 2000. Workers may use a line of silicon caulking material to divert water that runs over the face of the cliff onto ancient walls. On slopes where water can easily run downhill and undermine walls or wash away artifacts, workers cut down burned trees and use them

Slurry, dyed pink so pilots can see where they have dropped it, stains sandstone and takes a few years to wear off. The slurry dropped here at Step House didn't work. Fire damaged a significant portion of the trail and did some damage to the site as well.

to create water bars, log dams that deflect water around and away from archaeological sites. In many instances, excelsior matting is used. These mats of aspen wood shavings in a biodegradable plastic mesh slow the flow of water and provide a good medium for plants to take root. Burned trunks adjacent to ancient walls are removed so they won't topple in windstorms and rip out building materials on the way down. To prevent "root craters" from filling with water, crews stuff them with rocks and excelsior.

Natural erosion sometimes exposes human remains and sacred objects. In deference to the wishes of American Indian tribes, the park has committed its archaeological crews to reburying these remains and grave goods as close to their original location as possible. This responsibility is taken very seriously and carried out with the utmost respect.

Huge roofed, open-sided concrete shelters protect many of Mesa Verde's pre-Columbian features from the elements on Chapin Mesa's Mesa Top Loop and in Wetherill Mesa's Badger House Community. These shelters have heavy curtains that are pulled down in the winter to keep water from being blown in on the fragile sites, then reopened during peak visitation periods in the summer months. Unlike the alcove sites that have some protection from the elements, the delicate pithouses would quickly erode and fill in with sediment if left uncovered after excavation. In the early days of August 2000, when the Pony Fire threatened Wetherill Mesa, staff members hurriedly drew these curtains around the shelters to protect them from the fire front, then retreated to safety. The vinyl curtains slowed the flames, and in some cases actually stopped them from burning into the shel-

A good look at spalling. Fire superheats sandstone and the outer layer flakes off.

ters. However, the Plexiglas skylights of some shelters melted, allowing rainwater and ash to enter in the days and weeks after the fire. One pithouse did suffer some damage, although it was, thankfully, minimal.

The Badger House Community experience led to installation, at Pithouse B on the Mesa Top Loop, of new hurricane shutters which will be more protective in a fire. Budget permitting, Mesa Verde would like to install these shutters on the rest of the Mesa Top Loop and Badger House Community sites.

Temperatures in such extreme fires as Bircher and Pony may exceed 1,400 degrees Fahrenheit. Sandstone almost explodes when heated to such temperatures. Puzzle-piece fragments spall from the sandstone surface, leaving a weakened rock exterior that looks like "reverse measles," yellow splotches in the scorched black. Spalling can destroy the figures etched into the sandstone by early inhabitants many centuries ago. Such extreme heat damages the building stones of pueblos and cliff dwellings as well. In some instances, spalling on alcove ceilings may create a hazard for unsuspecting visitors, dropping sandstone chips on them.

TREASURES AT MESA VERDE

■ The park maintains a collection of more than 3 million artifacts, representing one of the largest archaeological collections in the National Park System.

■ The "type locations" for some of the park's primary stratigraphic layers were first described and named after formations in the park: the Point Lookout Sandstone and the Cliffhouse Sandstone of the Mesaverde Group.

■ The park has many fossils, some that are found nowhere else, including squid relatives, oysters, clams, sea snails, starfish, shark and ray teeth, fish scales and bones, dinosaur bone fragments, parts of marine reptiles and flying reptiles, palm fronds and trunks, petrified wood, jet, ferns, conifers, broadleaf trees, and other flowering plants.

7

THE 2000 FIRE SEASON
A NATIONAL PERSPECTIVE

Intense wildland fire is the result of many factors including severe drought.

T he 2000 fire season was one of the most challenging on record. In the midst of a severe drought, a series of storms produced windy conditions and millions of lightning strikes. The long-term effects of a century of aggressive fire suppression allowed the fires to become extraordinarily intense and widespread. Nearly seven million acres – more than twice the 10-year national average – burned throughout the West. More than a thousand homes within or on the edges of forests and wildlands were destroyed.

Twenty-nine thousand people were involved in firefighting efforts, including about 2,500 U.S. Army soldiers and Marines, and fire managers from Canada, Australia, Mexico, and New Zealand. Twelve hundred fire engines, 240 helicopters and 50 air tankers assisted.

A fire season of such magnitude reflects a long-term disruption in the natural

fire cycle, a disruption that increases the risk of catastrophic fires in our parks, forests, and rangelands in coming years. The 2000 season demonstrated what was possible with an exceptional buildup of fuel during a drought. Not everything burned that year and there are still hundreds of thousands of heavily forested acres that remain at risk. Even an end to the drought does not assure an end to high fire danger. After a fire season like the one in 2000, higher than average precipitation in burned areas will spur regrowth of grasses and low shrubs instead of trees. While fires in such vegetation are less intense, they move very quickly, carrying the fire to adjacent unburned stands of trees.

Settlement activity during the latter half of the 1800s upset natural fire patterns on a large scale. Millions of acres of forests and wildlands were cleared to make way for farm crops and pastures. During this time, timber companies often took the largest trees, leaving behind slash, undergrowth and smaller trees. Major fires resulted. In old growth pine forests of the type that are fire resistant, frequent low intensity fires keep the undergrowth to a minimum and don't harm the trees. As a result, there is no real opportunity for huge catastrophic fires that destroy whole

This panoramic view of the Bircher Fire taken from Mancos shows the magnitude of the fire and the scene residents faced for days on end.

forests. When loggers came in and clear-cut, they cut everything but took only the bigger logs. The branches, limbs and dead and down material they left behind on the ground were great fuel for a fire. The destruction wrought by such fires led to a policy of extinguishing *all* fires as quickly as possible. But in turn, that policy of suppressing all fires allowed dead and fallen trees to build up, further disrupting normal forest cycles and again setting the stage for major wildland fires.

Enormous growth of communities in rural and forested areas around the country, much of it in fire-prone areas and often adjacent to national parks and other public lands, has created what has come to be known as the "wildland-urban interface." But living in forested areas carries with it an increased risk of fire, leaving more communities and structures in harm's way. The National Fire Protection Association estimates that wildland fires destroyed more than 9,000 homes between 1985 and 1995. Officials estimate six times as many homes were damaged by wildland fire in the 1990s as in the previous decade. Wildland firefighters, accordingly, often spend a great deal more time and effort protecting structures than in earlier years.

The Cerro Grande Fire at Bandelier National Monument, a prescribed fire that raged out of control in the summer of 2000, was a striking example of what can happen when a fire moves rapidly into a developed area. Hundreds of residences were destroyed or damaged and more were threatened. This disaster greatly heightened awareness of urban interface problems, as did subsequent fires in Idaho and Montana.

The primary impact on communities surrounding Mesa Verde National Park is less related to fire threatening homes and much more closely tied to the area's economy. The topography and land ownership patterns around Mesa Verde have minimized wildland-urban interface problems here. Most of the fires at Mesa Verde are confined to one or two mesas. Because fire doesn't easily run downhill, fires that start in the park don't typically threaten the local communities. But when fires start on private land, as the Bircher Fire did, and then move into the park, fire's tendency to run uphill and up-canyon helps it spread.

Probably the most important outcome of the 2000 fire season from a national perspective was the national fire plan. Implemented in 2001, this plan called for a more organized and efficient approach to prioritizing fires, allocating resources, and looking at long-term solutions to heavy fuel-loading in many of the forests in this country.

8

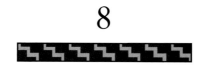

THE EFFECTS
OF WILDFIRES ON PEOPLE

Morefield Campground during the Bircher Fire. Firefighters lay out an intricate arrangement of sprinklers to protect the area from the approaching fire. As the flames advance, they survey their work and prepare to defend the structures.

 Fires at Mesa Verde have created an amazing spectrum of both positive and negative consequences on local and regional economies, on people in and around Mesa Verde National Park, and on the cultural and natural resources of the park. Mesa Verde National Park and the Durango & Silverton Narrow Gauge Railroad are the most popular destinations for visitors to Southwest Colorado. Tourism and the associated service industries are big business in Colorado and throughout the West.

The Mesa Verde fires of 2000 and 2002 in particular had a profound economic impact on Cortez, Durango, Mancos, and Dolores. News of widespread fires in the West caused concern among potential visitors to almost any area west of the Mississippi River. With the Cerro Grande Fire raging in northern New Mexico and the Bircher Fire taking off in Mesa Verde in 2000, countless people who had

Mesa Verde National Park

Bircher Fire 2000. The first few members of the incoming team assessing the fire, orienting themselves to the park at Far View.

planned trips to the Four Corners cancelled their vacations. The fires that seemed to engulf the entire region in 2002 had an even bigger impact. The local residents who run the hotels, motels, restaurants, and gift shops immediately felt the loss of revenue. Gas stations and grocery stores were soon affected as well. The economic ripples caused by the park closure were widespread. Unfortunately, when tourism is hit so hard and for as long as it was during the summers of 2000 and 2002, it takes a while to restart the economic machine. Bad news travels more quickly than good, and many potential visitors did not realize for weeks that the park had reopened, extending the economic downturn well beyond the actual park closure.

"I FELT LIKE IT WASN'T GOING TO STOP UNTIL THERE WAS NOTHING LEFT OF THE PARK I KNEW. "

Twice during the tumultuous summer of 2000, the employees of Mesa Verde were evacuated from their homes in the park. Many seasonal employees of the private, nonprofit Mesa Verde Museum Association, which sells books and other educational materials in the park bookstores, had to be laid off in 2000 and 2002. All park service employees kept their jobs, but those who resided in the park were moved into local hotels with only the belongings and clothing they could fit into their cars. Likewise, the employees of the park concession, ARAMARK Mesa Verde, were moved out. Many park service and ARAMARK employees were sent to other work sites during those hectic times. Rangers from Mesa Verde went to local visitor centers, welcome centers, and the Anasazi Heritage Center to explain the wildfire situation to both visitors and locals. Several park employees worked on the fire line or on support functions for the fire management organization.

For the people who know and love Mesa Verde, for those who have grown up in its shadow, the fires were both awe-inspiring and terrifying.

Those who worked directly on the fire were at least able to feel like they were contributing in some way. Working long hours day after day left them little time to worry about what might happen tomorrow. Nonetheless, everyone connected to Mesa Verde, even those working on the fire, had moments when they just stopped and wondered if it would ever end.

I write from experience. There was one day, well into the Bircher Fire, that I went out the back door of the fairgrounds building for a short break, and looked up at the mesa. Seeing yet another in the seemingly endless series of dark black clouds rising up into the sky, I just broke down and cried. I felt like it wasn't going to stop until there was nothing left of the park I knew. Never mind that the current summer was ruined for us, I wondered what our subsequent summers would be like.

Many of us knew most of the people fighting the fire. They were our friends, husbands and wives, parents and children, and some were trying to save their homes and offices as well as their park. Although the day would come when we might get excited at new discoveries in the fire's aftermath, it was the last thing on our minds. Some people's whole lives were up on that mesa. No one cared about new sites right then.

Day after day during the Bircher Fire, a fine rain of ash fell on the streets and homes of Cortez and Mancos. People as far away as Durango reported seeing ash in the air. Many local people said the ash rain was suggestive of a nuclear winter. Drivers on the highway leading to Mesa Verde could see flames shooting high into the air, devouring trees and bushes in their path. After dark, people in the Montezuma and Mancos valleys saw an eerie glow on the southern horizon. During the day, the huge mushroom cloud of smoke, dark and ominous, was a constant presence.

When the Pony Fire began burning in earnest to the west of the Bircher Fire, the common sentiment in surrounding communities was disbelief. Having two major wildfires in such close proximity of time and location was surely against the odds. The bizarre behavior of these fires terrified, frustrated, and confounded fire-fighters, locals, and visitors alike.

After several false starts in the evacuation for the Bircher Fire, there was no fooling around when it came time to evacuate for the Pony Fire. No one needed to be told twice and nobody dawdled. Most people still had their belongings packed and simply turned their cars around and headed back down the hill.

There are a few people who never came back to the park after that summer. The back-to-back evacuations were too traumatic for them. In a critical incident stress debriefing after the two fires in 2000, many people broke down as they tried to express their feelings. Part of it was, of course, the sheer exhaustion everyone felt after working so many hours for so many days in a row. It was hard to be rational and emotions were running very high. After the Pony Fire, there wasn't much summer left. It was only a few weeks until Labor Day weekend, the time Wetherill Mesa is generally closed down. In the hope of reestablishing familiar routines the superintendent wanted to reopen the mesa. Unfortunately, it was unsafe to do so. The dangers from falling trees, dust storms, obliterated trails, and alcove ceilings spalling were just some of the potential problems that had to be resolved before Wetherill Mesa would be safe for staff or visitors.

9

NATURAL RESOURCE
CONSEQUENCES

Mesa Verde National Park/Julie A. Bell

Fire spilled over from the mesa top down in front of Long House, and burned back uphill toward the site. Little was actually damaged though, because this spot fire was low intensity and was stopped by a stone retaining wall.

atastrophic events like the Bircher and Pony fires in 2000 inflict both immediate and far-reaching damage on the ecosystem. Day after day of intense, hot fires can cause a chemical reaction in the soil making it "hydrophobic," or unable to absorb any moisture. Fire and heat kill seeds in the soil and sterilize it so that many plants cannot resprout. The regrowth of a pinyon-juniper forest requires a certain sequence of events and it may be up to 100 years before those trees begin to reestablish themselves. Unlike grasses or oak brush, which can re-sprout from their surviving root systems, pinyon and juniper must reseed. The larger the fire, the farther the seeds must travel to fill in a burned area. Grass and brush seeds are easily spread by wind or animals, but pinyon and juniper seeds fall close to the parent trees. Some may be carried into the interior of a burn by animals, but pinyon-juniper forests generally reseed themselves from the edges of the burn inward. Unburned islands of trees inside the burn area help the process a little, but those seedlings only survive in the shade of well established grasses and shrubs.

After a fire, the first signs of regrowth are the bright green, nitrogen-rich small flowering plants and grasses. Fires usually occur during a dry period when indige-

Plant Life at Mesa Verde

At least 641 plant species have been identified in the park (93 are not native).

■ Rare endemic plant species occur on Mesa Verde that are found nowhere else. Some are rated by the Colorado Natural Heritage Program as Critically Imperiled Globally. Endemics include Cliff Palace milkvetch, Schmoll's milkvetch, Mesa Verde wandering aletes, and Mesa Verde stickseed. Other rare plants include maidenhair fern, Townsend's Easter-daisy, and the giant helleborine, a kind of orchid.

■ The park has champion-sized and very old trees such as a Utah juniper tree with a trunk 52 inches in diameter, largest in all of Colorado, and two others dated at 1,300 years old. Pinyon pines have been aged at over 1,000 years old and Douglas fir at over 800 years old.

■ The park supports a uniquely dense natural pinyon-juniper forest, some of the last and best intact old-growth pinyon-juniper forest left anywhere.

nous plants may be drought stressed. Very often the first signs of life after a fire are non-native grasses that are robust re-sprouters. Heat from a fire allows the soil to release nitrogen, and unless very intense heat has damaged the soil, grasses begin re-sprouting within a week. Shrubs follow, then gambel oak will sprout within a couple of weeks. Most of the others follow within a matter of weeks. Decades later, the juniper trees return, and last to grow – because they need shade to make a successful start – are the pinyon trees.

After the Wild Horse Mesa Fire on Wetherill Mesa in 1934, park employees attempted to plant 50,000 pinyon and juniper seedlings. Nearly every one of them died. The long, slow process must happen in its own time. In the areas burned by the Wickiup Mesa and Wild Horse Mesa fires, there are still virtually no pinyon or juniper trees to be seen 70 years later!

If a fire has been hot enough to steril-ize the soil and kill dormant seeds, exotic species often invade and take over burned areas. Big, bright purple-flowered musk thistle is Mesa Verde's most visible inva-sive species. While wavyleaf thistle, which has white flowers, coexists in moderate numbers with hundreds of other species, the musk thistle forms an increasingly dense mat, blocking many native plants and in turn depriving wildlife of their food supply. Invasive non-native plants also deprive the wildlife of cover. Cheatgrass is a low-growing annual that sprouts in fall and grows rapidly in spring. It browns out by June and then can burn readily. Cheatgrass easily invades the most damaged soils, for example, the circle right under a tree where the fire burned hottest. It gains a foothold in heavily damaged areas and how far it will spread is a matter of competition with other plants. The long-term implications are unknown, since the phenomenon is still relatively new for the park. Cheatgrass tends to promote re-burning since its own ability to spread is facilitated by frequent fires.

In a worst case scenario, these landscapes likely would remain weedy and self-perpet-uating, in turn fostering other problems. A weedy environment is prone to more ero-sion; the ground is unstable; the soil loses nutrients; and the environment has trouble

**Morefield Canyon before the Bircher Fire.
It was a typical pinyon-juniper mountain shrub community.**

**Morefield Canyon after the Bircher Fire.
Green islands in a burned area are common in a fast moving fire. Oxygen is sucked away
from those island areas by the fire on all sides so it doesn't burn.**

Mesa Verde National Park

These burned trees, called snags, can be deadly. The base and the roots are burned out making them very unstable. When the wind blows, they topple easily.

Canada thistle is an extremely aggressive, non-native plant that crowds out indigenous species, changing the forest. Aside from blackened trees and shrubs, this is the predominant feature now in the burned areas of the park.

supporting a woodland plant community again. It becomes a difficult cycle to break.

In an effort to combat the problem of invasive species as well as to forestall erosion, part of the rehabilitation plan is to reseed thousands of acres of charred mesa tops with native grasses.

The plant community is not the only one that will have difficulty recovering from fires. A lot of animals died in the fires, unable to outrun the flames. Some species, like rabbits and turkeys, are quite prolific and propagate rapidly. Many were lost but the rabbits especially seemed thicker than ever by the summer of 2004, only one year after the last fire.

Animals that like open country or edges of forested areas do well in burned areas, especially if good brush cover grows back to give them hiding places. Some deer are killed in a fire but others quickly move in, attracted by the new green foliage, which is especially flavorful and good for them. Deer are usually some of the first animals to return to burn areas, just days after the fire cools. They are browsers, not grazers, so after the new succulent grass is gone they will switch to leaves and forbs. Elk are grazers, more like cattle, and will do well in a burn area as well. Mesa Verde's elk population has grown over the last several years.

One family of cute little marmots in the park did not survive, leaving people to wonder if there will ever be a new family in the park. It would be a long way to travel for the chubby little mammals, especially because they seemed to prefer sun-

LIVING THINGS AT MESA VERDE

■ The park has recorded more than 1,000 invertebrates of many diverse groups, including the endemic Mesa Verde tiger beetle and the Anasazi digger bee. Many more collected specimens have yet to be studied.

■ The park has recorded 74 mammals, more than 200 birds, 16 reptiles, five amphibians, and 10 fishes.

■ The park was named an Important Bird Area (IBA) by the Audubon Society in Colorado mainly for its nesting peregrine falcons, Mexican spotted owls, golden eagles, and a suite of pinyon-juniper specialist birds.

ning themselves on the big flat rocks over any really strenuous activity. Many birds were able to flee but their habitat was destroyed and they probably sought out new homes. The burned trees do, however, serve a purpose, providing homes for many animals. For that reason, the park doesn't attempt to clear them all, preferring instead to let nature take its course – unless of course they are threatening to fall on a trail or roadway. Birds of the pinyon-juniper woodland such as the juniper titmouse, black-throated gray warbler, and pinyon jay, have lost considerable habitat so their numbers are down too. However, other kinds of birds that prefer open spaces have now moved into the park, including mountain and western bluebirds, house finches, and lark sparrows.

Animals that like dense forest have suffered and their numbers are down. Tree squirrels, Abert squirrels with their long tasseled ears, and red squirrels have dramatically declined mostly because so many Douglas firs and ponderosa pines have been lost. Researchers are in the process of determining the extent of the wildfire-related losses to the park's ponderosa pines, several rare plant species, and the threatened Mexican spotted owl.

10

KNOWLEDGE
FROM THE FIRES

From a narrow, human point of view, wildfires may seem catastrophic. The fires of Mesa Verde had devastating impacts on local and regional economies. Park residents were displaced, and some will never return. There is a certain hyper-awareness among most of the people in the park who have gone through fires here. When fire danger is high they really know it and most people take the evacuation plans and fire restrictions very seriously. Fire affected cultural and natural resources in both positive and negative ways. In the most holistic view, though, fire is neither bad nor good. It is simply a neutral and natural part of the larger ecosystem, an integrated system of people, plants, animals, and interactive natural processes.

It will be several years before a complete picture unfolds of the Bircher, Pony, Long Mesa '02, and Balcony fires' effects. Meanwhile, the 1996 Chapin 5 Fire offers a key, filled with the promise of tantalizing scientific knowledge.

The entire spectrum of human occupation of Mesa Verde, from the earliest Basketmaker sites through modern structures, was represented within the areas burned in the summer of 1996. That includes mesa top pueblos and villages dating from around A.D. 500 to 1300, sites that are generally less familiar to park visitors than the more famous cliff dwellings. Ceramic artifacts and sites of the Navajo people, dating from A.D. 1400 to 1600, were also affected by the fire. Corrals, hogans, wells, and windmills dating from the late 1800s to the present were within the burn area as well.

THERE WERE, HOWEVER, SOME SITES FOUND THAT BOGGLE THE IMAGINATION: A KIVA AND TOWER COMPLEX, AS WELL AS A SMALL COLLAPSED CLIFF STRUCTURE...

In three field seasons following the Chapin 5 Fire, archaeologists located an amazing 372 archaeological sites that had never been documented. It is almost inconceivable that there could be that many unrecorded sites. But considering the dense, nearly impenetrable vegetation covering much of Mesa Verde, it becomes more plausible. These "new" sites are not all of the magnitude of a Cliff Palace or Spruce Tree House. Many are small features – a wall, a single room, a series of check dams, or a small room block. There were, however, some sites found that boggle the imagination: a kiva and tower complex, as well as a small collapsed cliff structure that had been well hidden behind thick oak brush.

Given the abundance of sites revealed after the Chapin 5 Fire, it had been estimated that as many as 2,000 archaeological sites could come to light in the aftermath of the Bircher and Pony fires. Time and patient work will tell.

Out of the 1996 fire and the subsequent post-fire assessment and rehabilitation work came some discoveries that may ultimately change the way we view the early Mesa Verdeans. These people may have utilized a much more sophisticated system of water management than was previously thought. One and possibly two reservoirs were found in the burn area, bringing the total number of known reservoirs in the park to five – all at the same elevation. There were significantly more check dams in the backcountry than were known previously. One drainage revealed 105

FACTS ABOUT MESA VERDE NATIONAL PARK

■ Mesa Verde National Park was established on June 29, 1906, to preserve and protect the cliff dwellings and mesa-top structures of the Ancestral Pueblo people, formerly known as the "Anasazi."

■ Mesa Verde National Park is one of the best preserved and most concentrated areas of archaeological sites in the nation. More than 4,500 sites have been identified. Of these, more than 600 are cliff dwellings.

■ The park is probably best known for the cliff dwellings, Cliff Palace, Balcony House, and Long House. The archaeological sites in the park represent Ancestral Pueblo settlements dating from A.D. 550 to A.D. 1300.

■ The United Nations Educational, Scientific and Cultural Organization (UNESCO) recognized the park's international value and significance in 1978 through its designation of Mesa Verde as a World Cultural Heritage Site.

Acreage: 52,121.93
Federal: 51,890.65
Non-Federal: 231.28
Wilderness area: 8,100

check dams, creating a hillside of 105 farming terraces. Obviously, early residents of the area were maximizing their opportunities to grow crops in support of their ever-increasing population.

Ancestral Puebloans probably used fire to clear the mesa tops of vegetation in order to grow crops. Low intensity fire recycles important soil nutrients that are usually locked up in living plants, and makes these rich chemical compounds available to support food crops. Archaeologists theorize that the early farmers may have rotated their crops and used slash-and-burn techniques to ensure the continued fertility of the soil. Some modern farmers and ranchers in the United States still burn their fields. But the classic idea of slash-and-burn agriculture is really more a tropical forest technique where trees and shrubs come in rapidly after clearing. The rejuvenating effect of fire only happens one time in an area like Mesa Verde. Maybe a little pulse can be achieved during subsequent crop stubble burns, but there is a rapidly diminishing return from this technique in an arid area. Although we can only speculate, it is reasonable to presume the Ancestral Puebloan may have used this technique once in a while but probably got minimal results.

For two years following the 1996 fire, wild tobacco, which relies on fire to germinate, grew vigorously near archaeological sites. Tobacco is a sacred plant to many modern American Indian tribes and may have held a similar place in earlier cultures. Ancestral Puebloans could have used fire to encourage its growth.

Archaeology reveals only part of the story of the people and cultures of Mesa Verde. Much of what is known about the Ancestral Puebloans comes from other sources. The story of these people is found in the accumulated wisdom and knowledge of their descendents. Oral traditions of modern pueblo societies passed down through successive generation add color and humanity to data derived from the study of the material culture – architecture, artifacts, and landscapes. All these sources of information and insight can lead to understanding the lives and ways of the Ancestral Puebloans.

II

Consultation with American Indian Tribes

T he Native American Graves Protection and Repatriation Act of 1990 (NAGPRA) was a critical turning point in the relationships between the National Park Service and the people whose cultures are represented in the parks. This law requires that all federally funded museums and institutions that hold collections of human remains and associated grave goods return them to their modern descendents.

For the American Indian tribes associated with Mesa Verde National Park, the ultimate goal is to rebury these people and allow them to continue their journeys to the spirit world. Since 1993, representatives of 24 tribes have met each year with park staff to work out responses to NAGPRA that are mutually acceptable and beneficial to them as well as the federal government. Increased understanding and sensitivity among all are added benefits of the annual consultations between American Indian nations and Mesa Verde National Park.

The park's response to damage from the Chapin 5 Fire illustrates the ever-evolving relationship between Mesa Verde and the associated tribes.

Hundreds of years ago, Ancestral Puebloans pecked and etched dozens of figures into the sandstone surface of Battleship Rock, a butte in the upper section of Soda Canyon. The 1996 fire ignited oak brush and other vegetation that grew right up to the petroglyph panel. Superheated by the fire, the sandstone began to spall, taking with it pieces of the ancient petroglyphs. When experts suggested injecting a resin into the sandstone in an attempt to glue the remaining figures to the rock surface, the park staff asked for assistance from American Indian consultants. A small group of individuals came to the park, examined the panel, and listened to the scientists' suggestions. After considering the dilemma, these consultants requested that the park do nothing.

Although fuel levels were high, the Chapin 5 Fire was the result of lightning, a natural occurrence, they reasoned. It was their preference that the park service simply let the work of their ancestors erode naturally in the wake of this act of nature. The damaged panel was well documented with notes and photographs. Staff archaeologists did have a few pictures of the Battleship Rock petroglyphs before the summer of 1996, and these photographs became the baseline against which to measure the passage of time and the ravages of weathering. Each year a few more flakes of sandstone fall away from the ancient figures and the progression of erosion is documented.

The concerns of the American Indian descendents are respected and scientists have gained valuable knowledge of how sandstone petroglyphs respond to fires and subsequent weathering.

12

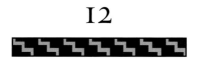

LOOKING BACK
LOOKING AHEAD

The aftermath of fire at Mesa Verde lasts long beyond the fires' smoke plumes.

 ire has always been part of the story of Mesa Verde. The park, its employees, area residents, and the visitors who were here during fire-stricken summers were affected in many ways. Their memories will fade, but never disappear completely. The cliff dwellings and other archaeological features were spared – this time. Plants and wildlife were dramatically affected, but nature will recover.

What should change is our outlook on wildland fire, our techniques for managing it, and our approach to living in the interface of wilderness and civilization. For decades, public lands managers have reacted to fires when they occurred, but done much less to prepare for or prevent the damage they can cause.

A former director of the National Park Service recognized several years ago that as a nation, the United States could no longer afford to manage fire purely in the suppression mode. Years of total fire suppression have resulted in an unnatural buildup of fuels that can feed catastrophic fires. Perhaps through the careful use of thinning and prescribed burning, it will be possible to restore a more natural fire regime to the land and its ecosystems.

The large fires of 2000, 2002, and 2003 provided Mesa Verde National Park an opportunity to continue working toward that goal. Beginning in the fall of 2002, park staff began preparation of a new fire management plan for Mesa Verde. It is hoped that the new plan will be implemented in the park's centennial year of 2006, melding the experiences and research of the past two decades into a more holistic and proactive approach to wildland fire.

FOR FURTHER INFORMATION

For information on Mesa Verde National Park, please look at the park website: **www.nps.gov/meve/** or write to the park:
Mesa Verde National Park
P.O. Box 8
Mesa Verde National Park, CO 81330
970-529-4465

For information on the National Park Service and fire management, please look at these Websites:
www.nps.gov
www.nifcjips.gov/fire/

An excellent overview of wildfires throughout the United States:
Fire in America. A Cultural History of Wildland and Rural Fire, by Stephen J. Pyne, 1982, Princeton University Press.

Fire ecology: *Ancient Piñon – Juniper Woodlands: A Natural History of Mesa Verde Country,* Ed. M. Lisa Floyd-Hanna, 2003, University of Colorado Press.

ADDENDA:
MAJOR FIRES IN MESA VERDE'S FIRST 100 YEARS

WILD HORSE MESA/WICKIUP MESA FIRES - 1934
Ignited: July 9 and 11, 1934
Total Acres Burned: 4,400

MOREFIELD FIRE - 1959
Total Acres Burned: 2,500

ROCK SPRINGS FIRE - 1972
Total Acres Burned: 700

MOCCASIN MESA FIRE - 1972
Total Acres Burned: 2,680

CHAPIN 5 FIRE - 1996
Ignited: Saturday, August 17, 1996
Contained: Thursday, August 22, 1996
Total Acres Burned: 4,781

BIRCHER FIRE - 2000
Ignited: Thursday, July 20, 2000
Contained: Saturday July 29, 2000
Total Acres Burned: 23,607

PONY FIRE - 2000
Ignited: Wednesday, August 2, 2000
Contained: Friday, August 11, 2000
Total Acres Burned: 5,240

LONG MESA - 2002
Ignited: Saturday, July 29, 2002
Contained: Thursday, August 5, 2002
Total Acres Burned: 2,601

BALCONY HOUSE COMPLEX - 2003
Ignited: Saturday, July 15, 2003
Contained: Thursday, July 20, 2003
Total Acres Burned: 2,730

NOTE: Total acres burned includes land within and adjacent to Mesa Verde National Park.

GLOSSARY

A

Ash flow: Ash washed off the burned area by rain, causing a flow that overwhelms natural or man-made drainages and floods roads and structures.

B

Backfire: A fire intentionally set in front of an advancing wildfire to consume fuel in its path.

BAER team: Federal Burned Area Emergency Rehabilitation team. Experts are drawn from across the country to assess the likely aftermath of catastrophic wildfires and prescribe measures to reduce property damage.

C

Canopy: Uppermost spreading, branchy layer of vegetation. Treetops.

Containment: Moderately aggressive suppression strategy designed to keep wildfire within the established boundaries of constructed fire lines. A fire is said to be contained when fire managers are confident it will not spread beyond natural boundaries and constructed fire line.

Control: Point at which a wildfire is declared controlled. A fire is said to be controlled when there is no risk of it increasing in size or spotting to areas outside fire lines.

Crown fire: Wildfire that jumps between treetops, independent of the ground.

D

Debris flow: Debris washed off a burned area by rain. Can include ash, mud, branches, trees, rocks, and boulders.

Defensible space: Natural or man-made areas where flammable materials have been cleared or reduced, forming a barrier between advancing wildfire and private property. A fuel break from which a fire can be more readily controlled. An area – typically a width of 30 feet or more – between an improved property, like a house, and a potential wildfire where combustibles have been removed or modified.

Drought: A moisture deficit severe enough to have social, economic, or environmental effects.

E

Extreme fire behavior: A high rate of wildfire spread, with prolific crowning and/or spotting, and strong convection columns. Unpredictable, erratic, often influencing the weather. Ordinarily precludes methods of direct control.

F

Fire behavior: How fire reacts to fuels, weather, and topography.

Firebreak: Natural or constructed barrier used to stop or check fires, or to provide a control line from which to work.

Fire line: Part of a control line scraped or dug to mineral soil.

Fire prevention: Activities – including education, engineering, enforcement and administration – directed at reducing the number of wildfires, the costs of suppression, and fire damage.

Fire retardant: Any substance, except water, that reduces flammability of fuels or slows the rate of combustion by chemical or physical action.

Fire shelter: Aluminized tent that reflects radiant heat and provides breathable air. Used as a last resort by firefighters in life-threatening situations.

Fire suppression: Attempt to reduce the intensity of a fire and ultimately extinguish it.

Flash flood: Sudden flood that follows rain. A danger after wildfires because burned areas no longer absorb as much moisture as before, resulting in faster and greater volume of runoff.

Forester: A person trained in forestry. A steward of the forest. One who studies forests.

Fuel: Combustible materials, such as dry grass, leaves, ground litter, plants, shrubs and trees, that feed a fire.

H-I

Helitack: Helicopters and crew used to carry firefighters, equipment, and fire retardant during initial stages of a wildfire.

Incident Command Team: Standardized on-scene management team trained to handle emergencies such as wildfires across jurisdictional boundaries.

L

Ladder fuels: Shrubs and low-growing branches on trees that allow fire to move with relative ease from the ground into treetops. When fires reach the tops of trees, they are much harder to contain.

Lead plane: Aircraft that makes trial runs over wildfires to check wind, smoke conditions, and topography and leads air tankers to targets and supervises their drops.

P

Plume: Smoke, heat and debris that build in a column above a fire. Columns can reach tens of thousands of feet in elevation, create their own weather, spawn fire tornadoes and kill birds in flight.

Prescribed burning: Setting fire to wildland fuels under controlled conditions that allow the fire to be confined to a predetermined area to accomplish specific land management goals. A prescribed fire reduces fuel build-up, prepares the land for new growth, helps certain plants and trees germinate, naturally thins overcrowded forests and creates diversity. A varied land and vegetation pattern provides a healthy habitat for plants and animals.

S

Slash: Debris resulting from natural events, road construction, logging, pruning, thinning, or brush cutting. Includes logs, bark, branches, and stumps.

Slurry: Liquid fire retardant, often colored pink, dropped from aircraft to slow or stop a fire's spread.

Smokejumper: Trained and certified firefighter who parachutes into wildfires.

Snag: Dead tree that remains standing, supported by other trees.

Structural firefighter: A firefighter whose training and specialty emphasize saving homes and other buildings from fire.

Suppression: All work aimed at extinguishing a fire, beginning with its discovery.

T

"Type" teams: Federal designations for firefighting teams. A Type 1 team has the greatest overall capability in manpower, training and experience. A Type 2 team is intermediate-level. A Type 3 team is often locally based. Type 1 or Type 2 teams may be brought in from out of the area. The teams comprise experts from all over the country brought together for fire suppression.

W

Wildland fire: Any unintentional fire impacting open lands, whether forest-, shrub- or grasslands.

Wildland firefighter: A firefighter whose training and specialty emphasizes suppressing wildland fires.

– Jim Greenhill

INDEX

R

red squirrels 94
regrowth 89
reseeding 93
reservoirs 99
retardant 56
retardant 5, 55
Rock Springs Fire 30
Rodeo/Chediski Fires 36
Romme, Bill 32
Roosevelt, Franklin Delano 29

S

safety zone 36, 43, 56, 60
Schmoll's milkvetch 90
sherd 66
sherds 65
silicon caulking 67
Skycrane 57
skylights 69
slash 59, 74
slash-and-burn techniques 100
slip-on pumper 30
Slurry 68
    reloading base, Durango 30
    staining 66
smoke jumpers 36
smoking 27
snags 92
Soda Canyon 67, 105
    5mv3758 67
    5mv541 67
    5mv542 67
soil, sterilization 89, 90
soot damage 65
spalling 65, 66, 69, 105
spike camps 66
sprinklers 36, 56
Spruce Tree House 34, 66, 67
Spruce Tree Terrace 66
stand replacement burn 41
Step House 68

Suppression 55, 73, 109

T

terrain 47
Thistle
    Canadian 93
    musk 90
    wavyleaf 90
thunderstorms 37, 55
tobacco 100
tourism 81
Townsend's Easter-daisy 90
tree squirrels 94
tree thinning 5, 32, 43, 55, 60, 109
turkeys 93
Type I Team 17, 19
Type II Team 19, 21

U-Y

U.S. Army soldiers 73
U.S. Forest Service 30-32
Utah juniper 90
Ute Mountain Ute
Ute Mountain Ute
    officials 6
    Reservation 17
    tribal land 20, 29, 37
Washington Post 19
waterfall 67
weather 47, 49
weeds 90
Wetherill Mesa 21-22, 29, 65, 68, 84
Whites Mesa 30, 51
    lookout tower and cabin 30
Wickiup Mesa Fires 29, 90
Wiese, Larry 5, 21
Wild Horse Mesa Fire 29, 90
Wildfire Situation Analysis 18
wildland-urban interface 75
wooden shingles 35
Yellowstone National Park 32